DARE
TO FLY

by the same author

Never Tell Me Never

JANINE SHEPHERD

DARE TO FLY

RANDOM HOUSE
AUSTRALIA

Random House Australia Pty Ltd
20 Alfred Street, Milsons Point, NSW 2061
http://www.randomhouse.com.au

Sydney New York Toronto
London Auckland Johannesburg
and agencies throughout the world

First published in 1997

National Library of Australia
Cataloguing-in-Publication data

   Shepherd, Janine.
   Dare to fly.

   ISBN 0 09 183505 4.

   1. Shepherd, Janine. 2. Crash injuries - Patients - Rehabilitation - Australia. 3.
   Skiers - Australia - Biography. 4. Air pilots - Australia - Biography. 5. Women
   air pilots - Australia - Biography. I. Title.

   362.43092

Design by Yolande Gray
Typeset by Midland Typesetters
Printed by Griffin Press, Adelaide

For the child within
who still believes
it is possible to
fly to the moon

And for Tim,
Annabel and Charlotte . . .
the wind beneath my wings

TO FLY

To soar and roam
to float and drift
to race, upsidedown
through a cumulus rift
to hug the profile of a mountain of white
A dazzling sculpture in shape and light
Climbing
Diving
Savouring life
Serenely thriving
on the priceless vision of a cloud-strewn sky
To be like the eagle
To fly
To fly

Jack Lynch

The only way
to discover
the limits
of the possible
is to go
beyond them,
to the impossible.

Arthur C Clarke

Acknowledgements

Once again, there are many people who have made this journey possible. Without them this book, and much more, would not have been possible.

I thank my husband Tim for his continued support and encouragement in whatever I do. Thank you for always believing in me. Much of this story is yours too.

I thank my two beautiful daughters, Annabel and Charlotte, for giving mummy the space needed to write my book ... most of the time.

I thank my parents, Max and Shirley and Tim's mother Marie for the endless days of baby sitting that have enabled me to juggle the demands of motherhood and writing. And thanks to my sisters, Kim and Kelley, for their friendship and support over the years.

I thank my dear friend Phil whose help at home has made my life much less chaotic.

I thank my friend Tony Peters, who once again came up with some great photos. Those early mornings are never easy! And I thank Debbie Peters, Godmother to Annabel, for her unwavering enthusiasm. Thanks, too, to Noel Kruse and all the crew at Sydney Aerobatic School, especially Joel, for their assistance with the photo shoot.

Thanks to Stephen Taylor, Charles Wooley, Mickey Breen, Nick Lee and everyone at '60 Minutes' for doing such a great job with my story. It was a lot of fun. I also thank all the staff at Prince Henry Hospital for allowing us to film within the hospital.

I thank my friend Adrian Cohen for his continued friendship, and for just putting up with me.

Thanks once more to Doctor Stephen for putting the other parts back together again.

I thank all of my 'old' friends who have remained my greatest supporters, and thanks to Pab for the poem that kept my spirits up in hospital and still makes me laugh. I couldn't ask for better friends. Thanks also to Les and Martha Nixon and Kevin and Babs Eastment for their friendship and words of wisdom which have always given me great encouragement.

I also thank Jack Lynch for his friendship and for allowing me to include his inspirational poem. Despite my best efforts to locate him, I could not contact Colin James, but I would like to thank him for his words which have helped me and which will continue to help others.

I thank my agent, Tony Williams, and Helen Rolland, Jeffrey, Sonya and Ingrid for all their assistance with my endeavours.

Thanks to the many people who have given me valuable advice and feedback in my speaking career, in particular Hap Hannan, Allan Morris, Amanda Gore, Christine Maher and Ron Tachii, who have spent endless hours talking to me and helping me refine my skills. Thanks also to Margaret Throsby and Gillian Armstrong for their support and advice.

I thank my friend, editor and publisher, Jane Palfreyman, for her enthusiasm, guidance and support throughout this project. Thank you for your encouragement in writing this book.

And I wish to thank, wholeheartedly, each person who has supported me in reading my story and to those who

have shared such intimate details in the letters they have
sent me. Thank you for allowing me to share your stories,
which will continue to uplift and inspire all who read them.
I am truly indebted to you.

Chapter 1

'COME ON, NENE , you can do it ... *Push*!'

I barely registered the voice. The pain was so extreme it was taking all my strength and concentration.

'Only one more hill, come on.'

My legs were beginning to weaken, and I found it almost impossible to lift my skis. I wanted to stop. I knew I should pull out; surely the others would understand.

I looked up, barely making out the Danish hill that loomed ahead of me. How on earth was I ever going to ski up it with such pain in my legs?

'*Push!*'

I could see a skier up in front. I was getting closer. If only I could catch her then maybe I could make it up the hill.

'Come on Janine, you love the hills! You can do it!'

The voices faded as I drew into myself. I could hear nothing but the rasping of my lungs as I pushed myself up the hill.

'Track!' I managed to yell as I caught up with the woman ahead.

She moved over and I skied past.

The pain was almost negligible now. I had gone beyond the pain barrier and my legs were numb. I was on automatic pilot. My head down, I looked up only to see enough to get me to the next corner. I didn't think any further than that. I couldn't.

No thoughts, just one leg, one foot in front of the other. Then I saw it. The finish line. It was flat all the way home. I pulled my skis together and began to double-pole.

One final push and I was over the finish. Just beyond the line, I collapsed. Not from exhaustion but because my legs gave way under me.

Someone pulled me to my feet.

'I can't walk,' I said. The pain had returned with a vengeance. With help I managed to get my skis off. My shins were swollen with blood, throbbing with pain.

I had finished; I wasn't sure how, but I had finished.

At the time I was unaware of the significance of that race, but now I realise it taught me more about myself than almost any other situation in my life.

I have asked myself again and again: Why did I push on despite the excruciating pain in my legs? Why didn't I simply pull out and save all the agony? That way at least I might have escaped the permanent damage I did to my legs.

The truth is, whenever I went training, if there was a choice between a flat course and a hilly course, I inevitably took the hills. I did it because I knew it would make me stronger. In fact, I ran so many hills, I actually learnt to love them.

So often in training I had run the hills, my legs heavy with fatigue, my heart pumping at maximum capacity. I could feel the ache in my chest as I struggled for air.

I loved that feeling and I have always loved the hills.

That was how I earned my nickname, Janine the Machine.

Not very flattering, but for me, for an athlete, the ultimate compliment.

Little did I know then how much I was going to need that strength. I was about to face the biggest hill, the greatest challenge I could have possibly imagined. And just like those hills in Denmark, I would again hear a voice saying, 'Come on, Nene, you can do it.' But this time it would come from inside, it would be my voice.

It was, after all, just another hill. And I love the hills!

Broken neck; back broken in four places. Broken arm, broken collarbone, five broken ribs, broken bones in the feet, head injuries, internal injuries, severe blood loss ... the list went on.

On a warm autumn day in 1986, I set out on a training bike ride with my friend Chris. We were to meet up with fellow Australian ski team mates for a ride from Sydney to the Blue Mountains.

As I waved goodbye to Mum that morning, my thoughts were only on the day ahead. That night I would be back home safe in my bed, no doubt exhausted from the day.

A split second is all it takes to turn a life around forever.

I was never again to return to that home.

Hit from behind by a speeding utility truck, my body was broken and my dreams and hopes shattered beyond repair.

It seemed so cruel; everything I had worked for, all that I had trained for, had suddenly been taken away from me. Instead of representing my country at the Winter Olympics—the dream of every athlete—I found myself in a spinal unit with extensive and life-threatening injuries.

After major spinal reconstruction and almost six months in hospital, I was sent home to my parents' new house in a wheelchair. Determined that nothing was going to beat me, my only thought was to get back on my feet as soon as possible.

But no sooner was I home than the reality of my situation and what I had lost began to sink in. In one cruel blow I had lost everything that was important to me. The doctors told me I would have to use a catheter for the rest of my life. I had permanent internal injuries and had lost sensation over my body and it would never return. At the very best I would need callipers and a walking frame. My life would never be the same again; I would have to rethink everything I did.

Why me? It was all so unfair.

I slipped into a very deep depression. Ashamed of my body, I felt utterly worthless. I spent a long time wishing things had worked out differently. I had lost all direction in life. There was nothing to look forward to, nothing to strive for.

With a bleak future and my self-esteem at rock bottom, I eventually realised that the only way I was going to beat this thing was to find something in my life to replace everything I had lost.

I had to find some purpose for living.

Even though the prognosis I had been given threatened to strip me of all hope, I believed that there had to be something that I could do. I couldn't give in to the cruelty of the situation. I had to run this race the way I ran the hills. Just keep hanging in there and sooner or later I would turn the corner and see the finish.

Sitting at the kitchen table with my mum and hearing an aeroplane fly over one day, the seed was planted.

'That's it, Mum,' I said casually, 'I'm going to learn to fly.'

'Oh that's nice, dear, don't you think you should learn to walk first?'

As ridiculous as it seemed, it became a driving passion. It was flying that was to get me back on my feet again. It was flying that was to become my dream.

I had nothing to lose so I threw everything I had into flying. At times I was terrified by the thought, what if I couldn't do it? But then again, I told myself, what if I could?

I gradually learnt to compensate for my injuries and be flexible in the way I flew. After many months of painful rehabilitation, my legs became strong enough for me to walk, if you could call my hesitant, lurching steps that, although the slightest puff of wind and I would have fallen flat on my face. However, the muscles, particularly in my calves and feet, had atrophied severely, which meant I was unable to stand on my toes and in the aircraft I was unable to put any pressure on the peddles.

In the early days my instructor worked all the pedals for me, but I knew I would have to be able to control the aircraft on my own if I was ever going to be able to go solo. Through trial and error I discovered that if I sat very close to the controls—too close for comfort for most pilots—and slid my feet up the pedals, I could push with the heels of my feet and use the strength of my quadriceps.

It was slightly unorthodox, but it worked.

When I started flying at the aerobatic school there was again the niggling doubt that I might not be able to control the aircraft in the air. You see, when you are four thousand feet in the air, and upside down in an aerobatic aircraft, you need to boot in a whole lot of rudder in order to turn the aircraft up the right way again. Now, controlling the aircraft on the ground and booting in a whole lot of rudder in the air are two completely different things.

It was a matter of trial and error again.

My first lesson was an aileron roll which is when the aircraft is rolled three hundred and sixty degrees round an axis in the air. My instructor, Noel, took me up and we attempted a few rolls only to find that I couldn't reach the rudder with my heels and get sufficient force on the pedals.

We adjusted the seat and added a few extra pillows, then I practised and practised and practised, until Noel finally said, 'How many times are you going to roll this thing, you're starting to make me sick!'

'As many as it takes,' I replied.

It took me a long time to get the timing right as my legs were very slow to react to my instructions. In fact, I don't have any lower leg reflexes so it was a matter of working out the best way of moving my legs so I could get the desired result.

I must have finally got it right because before too long I was teaching other students how to fly upside down!

Each new manoeuvre took time and patience to get right but flying aerobatics gave me an outlet for pushing myself as far as I could, to be the best pilot I could. It brought me back to life and gave me something to work for.

I might not have been able to walk properly, but that didn't matter, because I could fly!

Chapter 2

AFTER MY ACCIDENT I came to rely on my mum and dad for a sense of security; after all, they had nursed me back to health and knew all of my deepest insecurities. So getting married to Tim and moving out of their house was a big step for me, but moving hundreds of kilometres away just weeks after our first child was born was another thing altogether.

The move, however, was unavoidable.

At the time Tim was flying for a charter company based in Tamworth. His boss had kindly arranged for him to be based out of Sydney so that he could be close to home and fly the bank runs out of Bankstown Airport.

A very sad accident turned our lives upside down. One of the company pilots was involved in a fatal crash at Tamworth Airport. It was a severe blow for everyone involved as John was very popular and had only recently been married.

Tim was offered John's job. Although it would mean leaving Sydney, it would give Tim time on more sophisticated aircraft and increase his chances of one day getting into a major airline. It was too good an opportunity to miss and we took the transfer.

We packed up on our own, stupidly believing that we could cope. Tim's brother and his wife gave us a hand along with Mum and Dad. We packed everything up into a borrowed truck and trailer, and off we set, Mum and I in my small car with six week old Annabel in the back.

We arrived in Tamworth, unpacked as much as we could, and then Mum and Dad were on their way the very next day. I waved them goodbye with great sadness. I would be very homesick, I knew that.

I felt very, very lonely.

Without any delay we got ourselves into a routine. Of course this meant that Tim was off flying each day and sometimes at night, and I was left at home with Annabel. I spoke to Mum most days on the phone, not daring to think what the phone bill would be like.

Leaving the security of home also meant leaving the security of my doctors. It was important for me to find someone that I could feel comfortable with, but that wasn't easy. I knew my body extremely well; I had become attuned to its frequent problems. Whenever I came down with an infection, I would go to my doctor and get the necessary antibiotics to treat it. However, when I moved, I had to go through the entire procedure of explaining myself and my injuries over and over again, which was extremely frustrating.

Along with the regular infections and the resultant antibiotics that were a part of my life, there were other problems, in particular relating to my body's reduced sensitivity. On one occasion I had been for a swim at the local pool. When I was lifting myself out, I must have inadvertently scraped my leg on the side of the pool. Weeks passed, then one day I put my hand behind my leg when I was getting dressed and felt something strange. When I looked in the mirror I was horrified to see a large ulcerated area on the back of my thigh.

Mum drove me to North Shore Hospital where Adrian, my friend and former doctor, was working. The ulcer had become systemic and I was put on antibiotics and given some cream and dressings which Mum would have to apply several times a day.

It took at least a month to heal. That made me acutely aware of the problems I would face for the rest of my life and I made it a daily practice to check myself in the mirror.

Apart from my regular visits to the doctor, my time at Tamworth was mostly spent at home. I couldn't leave the house very often as Annabel did what most babies do—sleep. I wanted to get her into some sort of routine and didn't like to take her out too often. I decided that I needed to do something to keep myself busy and therefore committed myself to finishing my university degree.

After numerous phone calls to the university it was finally arranged that I would be able to finish my degree by correspondence. My lecturers were extremely accommodating and, knowing my situation, they went out of their way to be of help.

Although I was unable to finish my degree in physical education, I had accumulated enough credit to be able to complete a degree in human movement studies. I was unsure where this would take me but I just wanted to finish something. I had put in so much time studying over the years, it seemed a waste to let it go to nothing.

The relevant assignments were sent up to me along with any assigned texts and my days then became routine. In between feeding, bathing and playing with Annabel, I used what little time I had left to study. As Tim was working long hours, I immersed myself in my books, determined to make good use of my time.

The thing I really missed, however, was my flying. As I didn't know anyone well enough to trust leaving Annabel in their care, and because Tim was flat out at work, I didn't have any time to take an aircraft up and go for a fly.

I was intensely homesick and couldn't wait to go home for good. Months passed by very slowly and I finally completed all of the requirements for my degree. I also managed to renew my flight instructor rating before we left Tamworth. Tim had notched up quite a few hours on the Navajo aircraft he had been flying and we felt in our hearts that it was time to leave. The time spent in Tamworth hadn't been in vain but I was filled with excitement at the prospect of going home.

Back in Sydney and feeling at home again, the day came for my graduation ceremony. I could have had the degree posted out to me, but I had been through too much to do that. I wanted Mum and Dad to see me up on stage, being handed my degree; they had supported me throughout my studies and they deserved this just as much as I did.

It was strange turning up for my graduation day. I didn't know any of the people I would be graduating with as all my friends had finished their degrees while I was at home recovering from the accident. I hadn't attended any classes, so I had missed out on meeting any of the students from the same year. On top of that, I was there with my mum, my dad, my husband and my baby! It did feel a bit odd.

Despite feeling a lot older than the other students, I wasn't about to let anything stand in the way of enjoying the day. I wanted to savour the moment. I never thought I would be able to finish my studies, so it was a fantastic feeling to be there at all.

Mum and Dad were sitting somewhere at the back of the room with Annabel and my friend Debbie, who had been with me in my original course and said she wouldn't miss my graduation for anything on earth. When the allotted time arrived I managed to make my way up a rather large amount of stairs leading to the stage. I wanted to turn and wave triumphantly but I knew this would look a little out of place. Instead I shook the dean's hand, spoke a few words to him and moved off the stage.

I knew Mum would have a few tears in her eyes and Dad a great feeling of pride. I was the first in our family to go through university and what a struggle it had been to finish.

With my graduation over it wasn't long before I was dreaming up the next project. I suppose some people may have thought I could have been excused had I taken some time off and just enjoyed being a mum. I did enjoy being a mum; in fact, it was all that I lived for. However, since my accident I had begun to feel that there was no time to waste, and there were so many things I wanted to do.

I decided what I needed was a Diploma in Education so that if I ever decided to teach I would have the necessary qualifications. So it was back to the university, working out what courses I would need to complete the Dip Ed. I already had enough credits to fulfil most of the requirements so I would only need to study part-time over one year.

Although I was tired all the time, mostly due to my injuries, I was able to juggle being a mum to a small baby and studying quite well. I attended classes during the day and at least two nights a week, while Mum or Tim looked after Annabel.

When I finally finished the necessary courses, I was

required to go for an interview with a headmaster from a local high school before I could be admitted to the teaching list. Apparently this is a requirement for mature age students to ensure their suitability to teach.

My interview was arranged for a particular school located close to where I was living. I dressed appropriately, trying to look like a respectable teacher and presented myself for the interview.

After arriving at the school and being led into the principal's office, I was questioned about my course of study. The question that was most obvious, of course, was why it had taken me so long to complete my degree. After I had explained the forced break and detailed the accident as briefly as I could, the principal then went on to question me regarding my injuries.

'How do you intend to teach physical education to students when you are unable to perform the skills yourself?' he asked.

'Well, I don't believe the best teachers are those who are necessarily the best at sport. As long as I can get the point across, and use the other students to demonstrate, I believe I'll be able to teach quite well.'

'Perhaps, but kids can be very cruel as you know. How would you cope with them laughing at you and the way you walk?'

I was a little taken aback by this line of questioning.

'Well, I've been through so much, I know I could easily cope with any remarks from the students. I would probably just explain to them why I walk with a limp and what I've been through.'

I had never even considered that my limp might interfere with my ability to teach,' in fact, I hardly even noticed it anymore. I suppose I didn't fit the stereotypical image of a sports teacher anymore. My legs were no longer muscle-bound as they had once been. I knew I was different in many respects, but it still hurt to be reminded of it.

'I know that I would be a good teacher;' I said defiantly.

He looked at me and scribbled something down on the paper in front of him. I guess that must have satisfied him because he informed me that he was going to pass me.

And so, after ten years, I finally became a qualified physical education teacher.

Even if I never taught, what was important was that I had finished. It had been a long, hard slog, but it was one of my most fulfilling moments. It also made me aware that in the future I would have to prove myself in everything I did. From now on, I could take nothing for granted.

Chapter 3

WHILE I WAS STUDYING, Tim was flying whenever he could, working on a casual basis for different companies and being called out at all times of the day and night.

He was offered a permanent job flying the bank run down to Cooma, which he accepted. He would get up at four-thirty every morning and drive out to the airport to prepare the plane. Then he would fly all stops to Cooma, spend the day in a hotel room, then head back home in the late afternoon, getting home around eight at night.

It was a regular job as far as flying was concerned, but it was also a debilitating existence. Pilots were pushed to their limits to ensure that the mail got to its destination, and often this was at the risk of their safety.

For a while I had done some bank runs myself with a company out at Bankstown. I had been getting up some time in command under supervision—ICUS—on a twin aircraft. I mainly flew the Bourke bank run which took us to some pretty isolated strips. I loved the flying and the experience was great; however, being a commercial venture, you had to fly to the optimum to keep costs down to a minimum. This meant planning the most speedy approaches possible with the minimum turn around. You had to be fast and you had to be precise.

Times were logged and if you were continually slower than the accepted time for a certain run, you faced the prospect of being replaced. And if you weren't happy, there were hundreds of potential pilots waiting to take your place. Most of them would have worked for free just to get their hours up.

Some of the more enjoyable flights I spent cruising around in a Mojave pressurised aircraft. I did most of this flying ICUS with a pilot friend of mine called Michael. On the particular day we had the job of flying to Cootamundra to pick up Michael Willesee, who had a large horse stud there and often chartered flights. This was the first time I had been to Cootamundra and also one of the first times I had flown a pressurised aircraft so I was quite excited.

When we reached the airport, Michael and I prepared everything for their arrival. We had brought some fresh sandwiches for the passengers to enjoy on the flight home. We had also brought some liquid refreshment, as I had heard they liked a drink or two on the flight!

When Michael Willesee arrived with two other passengers he looked at me and asked 'You're not going to be flying this thing are you?'

I stood there, shocked. It was a bit of a novelty to see a woman pilot but I was stunned by his lack of tact.

'Um, well, actually, yes I am,' I answered, feeling more than a little defiant. Michael had heard Willesee's comment from the cockpit and turned around to see what was going on. Willesee motioned to him. 'Well, you just keep an eye on her then,' he said sternly.

I was all ready to defend my flying ability when I turned

to him and saw that he was smiling. He winked at me.

I giggled a little embarrassingly. He had only been kidding!

I closed the rear door and took my seat. Michael and I had a bit of a chuckle about it on the flight down to Sydney. The gentlemen obviously had no qualms about the flight because as soon as we took off, they got stuck into the booze and slept all the way to Sydney, waking just as we were about to land.

When we had completed all the shut-down checks, I left my seat and went to walk through the cabin.

'You didn't touch the controls, did you?' Willesee asked.

'You bet I did!' I said mock indignantly, knowing that he was having another go at me.

He smiled. 'Well, that's all right then. You did a good job.'

I actually think they enjoyed having a woman at the front—although I'm not sure how much they remembered of the flight!

On many occasions Tim didn't come home at the usual time and I would be worried sick that he had had an accident of some kind. So many pilots, many of them our friends, had been involved in fatal accidents, it was only natural for me to imagine the worst.

One night when I was quite pregnant with Annabel and feeling very uncomfortable, not to mention extremely emotional, I was home alone waiting for Tim who was very late home. He had been doing a lot of flying and I had been doing a lot of worrying. Of course I should have known better than to worry unnecessarily but with all those hormones streaming around my body, I was a wreck.

Then I heard on the news that a light aircraft had gone down at Bankstown. I immediately rang the Sydney Aerobatic School to find out the details. I knew a lot of people out there and I wanted to make sure they were OK.

No, I was told. It had been another aircraft from a different flying school.

The very next day there was another crash. I could hardly believe it. I rang the school again but no-one had any details. It was only a few days before Christmas which made the news even more tragic.

The phone rang in the evening and when I answered it I was relieved to hear it was Tim. He had landed and was on his way home.

'Hi,' he said. 'I have some bad news about the crash.'

'Who was it?'

'Boggie.'

Tim must have the facts wrong; he couldn't be right.

'No, it couldn't be Boggie.'

'He was with Peter. They were on a search and rescue for the aircraft that went down yesterday; there were six people onboard . . .'

I had stopped listening to the details. I didn't want to believe it. I was trying not to cry into the phone but it was impossible. I felt sick to the stomach.

In shock I hung up the phone and sat down. I couldn't believe that this could happen to a pilot of Alan's ability. Someone of lesser experience maybe, but not Boggie. He was a natural.

Boggie had taken me for my first aerobatic flight. He had shown me my first barrel roll, my first flick, my first spin.

'Do you want me to show you a spin?' he had asked enthusiastically one day as we continued to gain altitude.

'Sure,' I said.

'Ready?' Boggie asked at six thousand feet.

'You bet.'

Wham! Boggie pulled the stick back fully and simultaneously booted in full left rudder.

'Look inside or you'll get sick,' Boggie warned.

I did, but in my peripheral vision I could see the earth spin into a whirling blaze of colour beneath me.

I watched as the altimeter wound down rapidly; the aircraft was now in a stabilised spin. Boggie began to count down. '5700 . . . 5000, recover now. Hands off, feet off, identify direction of spin, full opposite rudder. Spin stopped, pull out.'

I could hear the engine start up as the air forced the prop to spin. It was a sound I would learn to love. I was hooked!

Boggie was the youngest pilot ever to be put onto FA-18's in the air force. He lived for his next flight. He flew anything; as long as it got up in the air, he was in it. He flew so many ultralights, he became an expert in forced landings—they're notorious for their engine failures. In fact Boggie must be the only pilot who has ever forced landed into Oshkosh, the famous air show in the United States.

Boggie was always dropping in on us on his way home from work, or on his days off he would come and just sit around. We all had some great times, getting up to all kinds of mischief.

Now he was gone. I just couldn't believe it.

I rang the school the next day, silently hoping that we had got it wrong. Perhaps Boggie wasn't on that plane after all. However, by now the news had filtered through aviation circles and the details of the accident were dreadful, too horrific to describe.

Boggie and Peter were the pilots in command. Peter was a good friend of Tim's; in fact they used to be flatmates. The two pilots had been flying up the valley when they had an oil leak which covered the windscreen. There was no visibility. There were only two survivors, neither of whom I knew but through a strange twist of fate one of them would become my good friend a few years down the track.

It was a great tragedy and many young lives were lost that day.

So perhaps I wasn't worrying unnecessarily when one terrible stormy night I began to panic when Tim, who had been doing a charter and was due home around eleven, hadn't arrived by midnight. I tried to ring the company to find his whereabouts but had no luck. Finally I got onto air traffic control—it helps to be a pilot and know who to ring!—and they told me he had left Melbourne hours ago and should have been home by now.

At two in the morning, beginning to get desperate, I managed to contact the company.

'Oh, I'm sorry. We diverted Tim on a charter to Brisbane, sorry we didn't contact you. He's landed back in Bankstown and should be home any time soon.'

By now any chance of sleep was ruined, so I decided to wait up. I waited and waited and waited. One hour passed and he still hadn't arrived.

Another phone call dispelled my worry but not my anger. Another charter had come up before Tim had a chance to leave for home and they had sent him off to Brisbane again. He must have been exhausted. He was well over his duty times. When he finally dragged himself home in the early hours of the morning, asleep on his feet, we knew we had to throw it all in. We just weren't willing to take the risks anymore.

There was a lull throughout the aviation industry around this time and it became so depressed that Tim found himself having to take any work he could find to earn a wage. Tim spent the best part of a year doing all sorts of odd jobs. He worked as a handyman and at one stage built a hotdog stand and began selling hotdogs at marketplaces. He even enrolled at university and began to study again.

Eventually he managed to get some regular part-time freight work flying nights out of Bankstown Airport which proved to be a pretty stressful time for us. Like many small-time operators, the company he worked for made it a policy to overwork its pilots and push them to the limits.

Aviation can be a very cruel industry, and every pilot out there knows that if they refuse to do the job, there are a thousand other pilots who will willingly take it on, despite the risks. Tim had a lot of pressure on him to keep flying and keep the hours up if he had any chance of getting into a major airline.

Flying night freight meant that he was sleeping during the day and flying all night. We really didn't see much of each other during this time—I would be waking up in the morning just as Tim would be arriving home and going to bed. At night I would go to bed, and the alarm would go off at around ten o'clock and Tim would get up and go to work.

As for me, I was about to embark on something that would open up more doors than I would have imagined.

I was sifting through the mail one day when a pamphlet caught my eye. It was a flier for a new club that was starting in the area, called Balmain Toastmasters.

I had only a vague idea of what Toastmasters was all about. However, my friend Hap had once been involved in it, so I decided to give him a ring. He had no reservations in extolling the many virtues of Toastmasters.

'It's the best thing I have ever done,' he said. 'You should definitely have a go, it's a fantastic organisation.'

After such high praise I said I would love to give it a go. And since it was so good, why didn't Hap come along with me? A little moral support wouldn't go astray. As it turned out, Hap did come along, and for that matter so did Tim.

The three of us went to the inaugural meeting which was held in a beautiful heritage cottage in one of the backstreets of East Balmain.

I hadn't been out socially very much since Annabel was born, mainly because I was too tired and I didn't like to leave her with anyone except Mum or Dad. I was quite protective I think! The night was a great success. The little cottage was packed to the brim. In fact, for some it was standing room only. We managed to find a few seats near the back of the room. Knowing the organisation taught public speaking skills, I thought it would be unwise to position ourselves too close to the front of the room!

The meeting began with a short introduction. Toast-masters was more than just a means of learning speaking skills, it was a place where you could learn to communicate more effectively, increase your confidence in public and generally improve your people skills. The speakers pointed out that it isn't just the high-powered executive who needs to speak in public; at some time in our lives all of us will probably need to stand up and speak to a group and, regardless of the size, we all need to be able to do this in an effective manner.

This all sounded extremely interesting to me. I was not sure what exactly I wanted to get out of Toastmasters. Partly I wanted to explore areas in which I had never really had any interest; having led what I now considered a narrow life as a sportsperson, I wanted to give everything a go. It was also good incentive to get out of the house on a regular basis. As much as I adored being at home with Annabel, I felt it important to maintain outside interests that had nothing to do with nappies or feeding.

The people organising the meeting explained the running of a typical Toastmasters gathering. They laid out the structure of the club and the titles of the office bearers,

which sounded a bit like the armed forces to me. One office
bearer was called the sergeant at arms and his job was to
make sure that everyone in the meeting stuck to the time
frame they had been allotted.

After all the housekeeping, the next part of the meeting
was called table topics. This is where you learn the skills
of speaking on your feet, without preparation. A few old
hands from visiting Toastmasters clubs demonstrated the
technique and they were remarkably good. One person
would give a prompt—a sentence concerning something
that might be, say, happening in the news—and then a
nominated person would have to come out to the front and
speak for one minute on the topic, without any preparation.

After the demonstration, us visitors were asked whether
we would like to have a go. As you can imagine, no hands
went up. Sitting next to Hap, I could see he was just itching
to have a go, but was just that little bit too nervous to put
up his hand. I couldn't resist, I put my hand up for him!

'OK, that gentleman sitting over there . . . You are a racy,
red sports car. Tell us about your life.'

Uh oh, I thought to myself, I think I'm in trouble! As
Hap stood up he glanced down at me with one of those
'you're really going to get it' looks but he fudged his way
through the minute. I'm not exactly sure what he talked
about, but that didn't really matter. He did a pretty good
job of it.

Before the accident, I had never had any time to do
anything other than play sport. This was my chance to do
something completely different. Before the meeting was
over, I had become the new Vice President for Membership
for the newly formed Balmain Toastmasters Club.

Within a few months the club was well and truly
established. Every fortnight Tim and I would drop Annabel
off with my parents and go to the meeting. We were issued

with our Toastmasters manuals and quickly learnt all about running a meeting and, more importantly, how to create an effective speech.

We met so many different people from such a wide variety of occupations that it always made for an interesting gathering. Some had come because they were required to talk in public at work; others came purely to improve their confidence.

The aim of the club was to finish all ten speeches in the manuals. Once I became friendly with all the other members, it was easy to get up and talk in front of them; it wasn't at all intimidating. After each speech, someone was given the job of evaluating you to see how well you had followed the objectives of that particular topic, the ultimate aim being to learn and improve. When the ten speeches were completed, members would become a competent Toastmaster, or a CTM.

The first speech in the manual is called the Icebreaker, and that's just what it is. As keen as I was to get started, I made my Icebreaker on the second meeting. I had taken down some notes, unsure if I would be able to speak for the required four to six minutes without them. As it turned out I didn't need them. I talked about my sport, my studies, and of course I gave a quick account of my accident. I didn't want to go into too much detail; I didn't have the time and thought it might be a bit disturbing. Nevertheless, when I finished I think most were a little shocked anyway. To look at me it was hard to believe what I had been through. When I wore a long skirt or dress, it was very difficult to tell I walked with a limp and of course, it was impossible to see my internal injuries or my scars. So when I told people I was a partial paraplegic, they just looked at me in disbelief.

My Icebreaker was the beginning of a new vocation for me, although I didn't know it at the time.

Chapter 4

I BEGAN TO MISS my flying terribly.

I had been spoilt teaching aerobatics; not only had it given me a wonderful feel for flying and considerable confidence with the aircraft, it was also great fun.

In fact, it was so much fun that we all got up to a bit of strife some time or another in our teaching careers. I remember one day very clearly when I was up flying with Boggie; we had some time off and thought we would go do some aeros.

While we were out in the training area I recognised the voice of one of the other school's pilots on the radio.

'Let's go and say hello,' Boggie said when I told him.

I knew he didn't mean via the radio but wasn't quite sure what he had in mind.

Next thing I knew Boggie had the controls and we were pulling close to the other aircraft. Suddenly he pulled up into a barrel roll and over we went, right over the other aircraft! We finished the roll and came up alongside our friends. I gave a little wave; what else could I do? I knew we would get into trouble as soon as we got back, but with Boggie it never seemed to matter, he had such nerve.

As expected, when we landed the boss summoned us into her office. She had already had a call from the chief flying instructor from the other school. I had to plead innocence— I had no idea what Boggie was going to do. Boggie, in his typical manner, just saluted, apologised and promised never to do it again.

Noel from the Sydney Air School had trained Tim and Rob in formation flying and we often went out to do some formation. We were amazed at the teams the other flying schools had assembled. They were absolutely terrible. The aircraft were miles away from each other and the flying was very sloppy. Tim, Rob and Noel, on the other hand, flew an extremely tight formation. It was just wonderful to see. Actually, everything about SAS was extremely professional, largely due to Noel's air force background. He was a great teacher and it wasn't until I flew at SAS that I really learnt to fly.

Flying formation well is extremely demanding. You have to be on the ball all the time, watching for any minute changes to speed or altitude. Noel also taught Rob and Tim formation landing and takeoffs, which not only impressed me but the blokes in the tower as well.

I was next in line to start formation training when I fell pregnant, so unfortunately I didn't quite make it. But it is something I want to do in the future.

I remember flying at SAS with great fondness. After all, that is where I met Tim! I recall my friend Jack, also an air force pilot, telling me that to fly well, you have to feel at one with the aircraft. Your arms have to be extensions of the wings of the aircraft and you have to feel this through your hands and the stick.

As much fun as I had had with the school in the past I

knew it was time to move on. I didn't want to instruct on a full-time basis because it would have taken me away from Annabel for long hours, so I was forever trying to think up ways I could fly part-time.

Owning an aeroplane, I decided, would be the perfect solution. That way I could fly whenever I wanted and when I wasn't flying I could put it on line with a flying school. I could run the aircraft like a business and get some sort of income to at least pay the running costs.

I wanted an aerobatic aeroplane that I could have some fun in but one that could be used for training as well. I would have liked to have been able to afford a bi-plane, like a Pitts special, but it would have been far too impractical.

Any ambitions I might have had of one day competing in aerobatic competitions had long since vanished. I just couldn't afford the luxury of spending large amounts of time, let alone money, on the practice needed to compete. To be at all competitive you need a good aeroplane, which costs a massive amount of money, and on top of that you have to pay for the fuel every time you fly. Consequently, the field is small and includes the very rich who can indulge in a luxury sport, and a small group of other pilots who have access to a reasonable machine.

I searched around and decided that the best aeroplane for me was a Victa Airtourer, an Australian-built aerobatic aircraft very similar to the Robin aircraft I had been teaching in. It would be a good little trainer and it would be ideal both for aeros and to go cross-country if needed.

Through the grapevine, I heard that the New Zealand Air Force was selling a fleet of four Airtourers that had been used for training. The aircraft for sale were actually called T-6, which is the military version of the Victa. They are slightly bigger than the standard Victa and have a bigger engine. They had been kept in a hangar since their production and therefore would be in excellent condition. The Air Force was calling for tenders from overseas and the top bidders would acquire the aircraft in bidding order.

I sent away for the relevant details and then had to do some inquiring around about what they were worth. I rang as many informed Victa owners as I could to compare aircraft types and to place some realistic value on the T-6s. I eventually came up with a price and sent my offer off to the New Zealand Air Force. Then I waited.

I was delighted when some weeks later I heard I was going to be the happy owner of one now ex air force T-6. I was the owner of my first aeroplane! My joy was somewhat offset by Tim's reservations. He believed there was nothing as troublesome as owning an aircraft. However, he knew better than to question my judgement and let me go my own way on this.

There was so much red tape to go through before the T-6 could even leave the ground in New Zealand; in fact, so much expensive messing around that I began to wonder whether I should have listened to Tim after all!

Before the plane could leave New Zealand, we had to choose a call sign for it to satisfy Australian regulations. I searched through the list of available registrations and decided to call my aircraft Mike Uniform Mike or MUM. I thought it was very appropriate!

We decided flying it over to Australia would be the least expensive option and it wasn't difficult to find someone keen enough to fly a single engine aircraft over that expanse of water, especially since they would be getting paid for it.

We made all the arrangements for one of the pilots from Tim's old company in Tamworth to fly MUM over and since there was another T-6 coming to Australia, they would fly together.

When they finally made it to our soil, with all the hiccups and paperwork behind them, we arranged to have the original air force markings put back so that it could retain its original character.

During the entire process of buying and acquiring MUM, we had the most wonderful news regarding Tim's work. He got a job with Eastern Airlines. We could hardly believe it. After all the effort Tim had put in over the years since he had begun flying when he was sixteen, this was finally the break he was looking for.

The aviation industry is one of the toughest around. There are so many hopeful young pilots trying to fly for a large commuter airline, but there are very few jobs available. We had been so close to Tim throwing it all in. In fact he had only recently completed a course that would enable him to enrol in aeronautical engineering at university. Now there was a light at the end of the aviation tunnel.

No longer would I have to sit at night wondering if he would come home. No more shonky charter companies or operators. Easterns was a good little operation, and as it wasn't a part of the general aviation industry, but was RPT, or regular public transport, it meant Tim would finally have a roster and we would be able to plan our lives instead of always waiting for the phone to ring.

We flew with Eastern Airlines up to Tamworth to pick up my little MUM so that we could fly her back to her new home in Bankstown. Seeing her for the first time was wonderful. She looked exactly the same as she had when I first set eyes on her in the original photographs.

Being an old aircraft, she was a bit worn out inside, but that was what made her so full of character. All the blokes in the hangar that had been working on MUM thought she was beautiful, and so did I.

I couldn't wait to get in and fly her home.

Once MUM was established at her new home, it was a matter of locating her with a school so that we could earn some money to pay for her expenses.

We couldn't afford to hangar MUM, so that meant she was left out in the open, come rain, hail or shine. At first I wasn't overly concerned by this but when I actually saw my little 'baby' out there, sitting on the tarmac in the rain, I felt as though I should cover her up to protect her!

The next step for me was to get back into flying and teaching. I felt I was pretty rusty so I spent some time flying MUM to get up to scratch and to familiarise myself with my own aircraft.

I had initially had MUM on line with a particular school; however, like any typical mother, I felt she wasn't being looked after well enough. Without hesitation I put her on line with another school where I believed she would receive more TLC.

My first student was a friend of my neighbours. They had told me their friend from Korea was an absolute nut about flying. When I finally met him, he was over the moon at the prospect of learning to fly and quickly asked me to teach him the fundamentals.

Had I known what I was getting myself into, I might have thought twice before I agreed.

Lesson one. We met out at the airport. I took Francis into the briefing room to run through the things we would be doing in our first lesson.

'Right, let's have a look at the different parts of an aircraft,' I said as I held up a model aircraft and proceeded to show him the different control surfaces.

He had a grin on his face the entire time I spoke to him. After half an hour of talking and deciphering what I could from his answers, which was made difficult by his thick accent, I decided that he must have taken some of what I had said in so we might as well go flying.

We walked around MUM to complete the pre flight; Francis was following me very closely, with that grin glued to his face. Whenever I asked him a question he would answer, 'Oh, I forget, sorry', and then just keep grinning.

I realised this wasn't going to be easy and in fact it went from bad to worse. I had always firmly believed that anyone can fly, but now I think that there are always exceptions to the rule!

We spent the entire week slowly making our way through the first lessons in the private pilot's syllabus. Francis never seemed to listen to what I was telling him because when we were in the air he had no idea of how to pole the aircraft. In fact, I was convinced that he was actually trying to kill me!

I decided to call it quits when we were in the briefing room one day, taking a much-needed break from our lessons, and Francis began questioning me about his licence. He wanted to have a look at mine.

I took it out to show him. He was stunned.

'Where is the photo?' he asked.

'No photo, that's it,' I told him.

'Oh, I want a photo on my licence, to show my friends.'

I suddenly realised that the only reason Francis wanted to fly was to get the little piece of paper at the end so that he could take it out and impress people. That explained a lot of things!

Francis went home to Korea but said that he would be back to pick up where we had left off. Fortunately for me, the disappointment of not having a photo must have been greater than fulfilling his need to fly because I never heard from him again.

MUM did some more flying out at Bankstown, but after

only one year Tim and I came to the conclusion that
owning an aircraft was definitely not a wise financial
decision. Well, Tim had long ago come to that conclusion,
but I had been far too stubborn to admit it.

We put her up for sale, and before long we had a very
keen buyer who wanted to purchase the aircraft for their
flying school in, of all places, New Zealand.

We bade her a sad farewell and as MUM took to the
skies and returned to her Kiwi home, I thought I would
never see her again. But as it would turn out, I would be
reunited with her once more.

Chapter 5

I CONTINUED TO stay in close contact with Elizabeth Etherington, the woman to whom I owe my life. Had it not been for her timely arrival at the scene of my accident, I certainly wouldn't be walking today. We have become very close friends and I consider her to be my soulmate.

When I first decided to learn how to fly, I had no idea where it would take me. I didn't even know if I would be able to pass a medical! After I had successfully completed my tests and flying for my Restricted Private Pilots licence, I proceeded to complete the requirements for the Unrestricted Private Pilots licence.

This included a number of cross-country flights to teach the skills needed to navigate an aircraft from point A to point B. I was very excited to find out that one of my flights was to take me to Mudgee, where Elizabeth lived.

I decided to surprise her. I called her and told her that a pilot friend of mine was flying to Mudgee in a week's time, so I thought I would go along for the ride so that I could pay her a visit.

Elizabeth had no idea that I was learning to fly so I couldn't wait to see her face when she realised I was flying the plane!

The last time Elizabeth had seen me, I was a battered mess lying on the side of the road. When the ambulance drove away that day, she never thought she would see me again. Indeed, my injuries were so extensive, the doctors thought I would certainly die.

When Elizabeth and her husband Larry were travelling home to Mudgee that weekend with their friends, the last thing they expected was that they would be involved in a near fatal accident. Elizabeth had been so moved by what she had witnessed that day, she had written a poem which she sent to my mother. It is a wonderful, moving poem that evokes incredible emotion in me every time I read it.

When my mother received the poem in the hospital and read the name at the bottom, she couldn't believe it. Elizabeth and Larry had been friends of my parents years ago. It seemed an amazing coincidence.

We made contact with them and they were just as shocked to discover the connection. Of course they had no idea who I was; they had just sent the letter to the hospital in the hope that my mother would receive it.

The trip to Mudgee was one of my early navigation flights, so I took more than ample time to get everything right before I took off. This was as much to reassure my mother as anything else—she was always a bit nervous, but I guess I couldn't blame her after what she had been through since my accident. But she knew better than to curb my enthusiasm; she knew I just had to fly! I did all of my preparations at the briefing office, and then conducted a thorough pre-flight test on the aircraft. As I took off from Bankstown airport, I relished the feeling of being in the cockpit all alone. It was great to fly solo in the training area, but it was something else to actually leave the area and head on out over the mountains into the great expanse ahead. Total freedom!

I was extremely fanatical about my maps and procedures, I had carefully done all the preparations and I felt fully confident. As I flew over the Blue Mountains, I glanced down to see the road on which I'd had the accident. I could see all the cars speeding up the insignificant looking, winding mountain road, and shivered at the memory of that terrible day.

All I can recall is the cold air on my face. The day remains a blur. I remember setting off from home, kissing Mum, and then heading off to tackle the mountain ride. I would be home later that night, after a good ride and a hearty meal.

Or so I thought.

To set about doing what you normally do, a routine activity like walking or driving to school or work, and then to wake up in hospital with no memory of what happened—is a nightmare. That is how mine began.

When Mum and Dad were called up to the hospital they had no idea how serious my accident was. My friend John didn't want to panic them so he avoided saying just what my injuries were.

I was taken to Katoomba Base Hospital from the scene of the accident. When Mum and Dad arrived at the hospital they were shocked to say the least. There was a young doctor there who had just arrived from London to his first permanent placement. When I landed on the doorstep, I don't think he could believe it either. It was really a case of being thrown in at the deep end.

Mum and Dad were not allowed to see me straight away.

Mum said all she could see were my feet sticking out from under a sheet, as medical staff fussed around me.

She overheard someone say, 'We can't stabilise her blood pressure'. For any parent to be called in to see their child like this is the worst kind of nightmare.

The doctor approached them and offered Mum some sedatives. She knew then that they were expecting the worst, but refused the sedatives, wanting or needing to be awake if the unthinkable happened—if I died.

The helicopter landed in the nearby oval to take me to Sydney. They took me out into the cold night air to load me onto the helicopter. This must be when I felt the chill of cold air on my face.

They loaded me onto the chopper and Mum and Dad began the long drive down to Sydney to meet me at the hospital, not knowing whether they would ever see me alive again.

The helicopter crew did their best to keep me alive during the flight. The blood loss was so extreme they didn't think I would make it. On arrival at the hospital, my blood pressure had dropped to 40 over nothing. It was an emergency situation. One doctor who had seen me being taken away recalled later how he had heard another doctor say to him, 'Oh well, you win some, you lose some.'

I had only just begun the fight.

It was astonishing to think that I was recalling this trauma from the cockpit of a plane I was flying. Looking ahead I could see the ground stretching far to the horizon. I looked down at my maps to confirm where I was going, giving my call to flight service, making sure I observed standard procedures, and then set my compass and new track to head to Mudgee.

After landing at Mudgee Airport, I taxied the aircraft over to the parking bay and glanced at my watch. I was early. I looked around and couldn't see Elizabeth, disappointed that she hadn't seen me land. I shut the aircraft down, secured it and then got out to see if I could see her coming.

Eventually I saw a car approaching. By now I was standing over near the gate, well clear of the aircraft. The car stopped and Elizabeth jumped out. She ran over and gave me a big hug.

'It's great to see you. You look fantastic,' she said.

'Thanks, you look great too,' I beamed. I knew what was to follow.

She looked around. 'Where is your friend?'

'Well, actually, there is no friend.'

She looked confused.

'You see, I flew myself here. I have been learning to fly.'

She was incredulous. 'What? I don't believe it, I just can't believe it . . . ' She shook her head in disbelief. 'Last time I saw you I didn't think you would live, let alone walk . . . And now you can fly.'

Elizabeth took me back to her house for lunch and to see Larry. It was an extraordinary coincidence that they knew Mum and Dad but even more bizarre was the fact that in the course of conversation Elizabeth and I discovered that we shared the same birthday. We really were soulmates.

It is actually Elizabeth who has filled me in on much of what happened at the scene of the accident, for I have no memory of it. She recently told me that when she ran from the car to my side, the lady she had been travelling with followed her. However, her friend took one look at me, vomited, and had to return to the car. Elizabeth told me that I was the most horrific sight she had ever seen. As she sat beside me on the roadside waiting for the ambulance, she wondered how anyone could possibly survive such horrific injuries.

I recall some of the poem;

There'll be many times when we'll look back upon that fateful
  day
When life gave to all of us a reason why we pray.
To many it may be very hard when life is hurt so deep
But with the days of passing time think of all the love she'll reap.

Time has passed, and I know it is only because of the healing power of love and friendship that I have made it this far.

Chapter 6

WITH THE TOASTMASTER'S Icebreaker out of the way, it was time to move on to the second speech in the manual. This time it was up to me to choose a topic. I was required to talk for between five to seven minutes, which seemed like an eternity.

After much thought I decided to talk about spinal injury awareness; after all, this was something I had first-hand knowledge of. Each speech has a purpose and this one was to convey sincerity and earnestness to the audience, hence the topic 'Be in Earnest'.

I rang the Australian Quadriplegic Association, which I was a member of, to ask if they could send me some statistics. I also rang Adrian to see if he had any information he could send me.

I spent a lot of time constructing my speech which I organised into little pieces of paper that fitted into the palm of my hand. I was going to attempt to speak without notes, but thought I should keep some with me just in case I got stage fright.

When the time came and I was finally called up to the lectern, it was surprisingly easier than I had anticipated. I had researched my subject well enough to feel confident in conveying my message, and I felt that what I was saying was worth hearing.

Even I was surprised at some of the statistics I had dug up. Adrian had sent me a paper documenting research into treatment immediately after an accident and the incidence of permanent spinal injury occurring as a result. It showed that most cases of paralysis actually happen as a result of mismanagement at the scene of the accident. This is due to a lack of awareness by the public and health care professionals. Those who reach the accident first obviously believe that by removing the person from the scene they are doing the most good; however, often they are in fact damaging the spinal cord permanently.

The paper showed that as high as twenty-five per cent of people with permanent spinal injury were paralysed as a result of mismanagement. What a terrible price to pay for ignorance.

This knowledge made me even more grateful for Elizabeth's timely intervention at the scene of my accident. When she reached me there were a few young men with their hands under my arms about to lift me up into the front of a utility.

'Hey, what are you doing?' Elizabeth screamed.

'We are taking her to hospital,' was their reply.

They obviously thought they were doing the correct thing, but in fact I very nearly became the one in four statistic. Had Elizabeth not intervened I would never have had any chance of walking again.

I gave my speech with a great deal of enthusiasm, thinking perhaps someone listening might need this information in the future. I finished with a detailed account of how correctly to manage a potential spinal injury victim at the scene of an accident, stressing that *all* victims of accidents should be treated as potential spinal victims.

Needing my notes only a few times throughout the speech, I felt fairly pleased with my performance, but even more pleased that I had loads of room for improvement.

Working my way through the manual, I started to enjoy having to talk about topics that I knew little or nothing about. It gave me the opportunity to research and learn things I would never have otherwise become involved in.

Not long after I joined up I volunteered myself for a speaking competition. There were three different competitions within the Toastmaster organisation—the humorous speech, the international speech and one for the evaluators. The international speech competition was the big one, the serious one, and the winner would go to America to represent Australia in the World Championships of Public Speaking.

I wound up volunteering for our local club's humorous speech, mainly because my friend Hap talked me into it. We needed the numbers, he convinced me, or there would be no competition. I was a bit hesitant as I had never thought of myself as funny and wondered what on earth I would speak about.

After much thought I decided that I should give a talk about what happened when I took four friends outback on a flying trip that ended up in a place called Windorah when I was forced to deviate from my course to Charleville due to bad weather. I only had five to seven minutes to tell my story, which isn't long for such a complicated yarn. I decided I would have to make the introduction very short and get to the punchline quite quickly, with lots of funny anecdotes along the way.

My biggest problem was that my story was really about

the lady we had met in Windorah, Bubs was her name. When we landed the aircraft, relieved at last to see land with night approaching fast, we were approached by a rather large woman.

The Dude, an American travelling with me, was busy kissing the ground when Bubs approached.

'G'day,' she said. She looked quite threatening. Not the sort you would want to meet down a dark alley.

'What sort of plane is this anyway?' she growled.

'Oh, it's called a Trinidad,' I answered.

'I'll just call it shit for short,' she bellowed.

I just nodded. Anything she said was OK with me.

I decided to introduce ourselves. 'My name is Janine, this is Meredith and this is the Dude,' I said, holding my hand out.

She almost crushed my hand, then looked at the Dude. 'You can call me Bubs, and I'll just call you Shithead,' and she roared with laughter at the joke.

Well, it was funny at the time. The problem was how to tell the story to an audience. You see, it wasn't considered polite to say words such as 'shithead' in a professional capacity, even though it was a direct quote.

Hap and I had talked about it and we came up with the idea that I should use something to take the place of saying the words in the speech. Hap had an old bike horn which would do the job perfectly. The idea was that, at the appropriate time, instead of saying the rude word, I would honk the horn instead. Hopefully the effect would be funny.

The night arrived and I was a little nervous, worrying about whether or not the audience would laugh. It would be embarrassing if no-one responded, or if the horn was a flop. Oh well, it was too late now.

Hap was busy going over his speech and the lack of conversation between us was a dead giveaway.

'What are you speaking about?' I finally asked.

'I'm speaking about men's experiences in supermarkets.'

I couldn't believe it. 'You mean you're not talking about the Great Hoover Sweep?'

I had first heard this story when Tim and I had been living in Tamworth. We had checked our answering machine one day to find a message from Hap. It went for about ten minutes. It was the funniest story and Tim and I sat there listening to Hap and laughing our heads off.

Hap is one of those people around whom unusual things always happen. For example, one day he had parked his car near The Rocks market in Sydney; when he returned to his car later that day, he found a big imprint of a body on his car. Someone had tried to jump off a bridge and landed on his car. It could only happen to Hap!

The Great Hoover Sweep was another story.

Hap looked at me blankly. 'Oh no, I had completely forgotten about that.'

'You have to do it,' I implored.

'I can't change it now, it's too late to make up a speech on the spot.'

'Oh come on, Hap, just tell the story the way you told it to me; it's hilarious, you have to.'

He started to panic; we only had a few minutes until the competition started. But if anyone could speak off the top of his head, it was Hap. He had the gift of the gab. We were number four and five on the list, so he had at least twenty minutes to construct a speech, although he would have to do it in his head while someone else was giving a speech. It wasn't exactly ideal preparation.

My turn came and I walked up to the front of the room. I had decided to wear flying garb: a flying jacket that had been presented to me from the Westpac helicopter team, a leather flying cap and some headsets. I probably looked absolutely ridiculous, but I didn't care. I just wanted to have fun.

I began my speech, entitled 'Windorah or Bust'. The atmosphere in the room was jovial, everyone was there to have a good laugh, and that gave me confidence. When I reached the part with the horn I squeezed hard and all that came out was a pathetic little squeak, not the loud bellow it had given in practice.

It didn't matter though, everyone laughed. I made it to the end of the speech and was relieved when I received a good response. It wasn't that hard to be funny after all.

Now it was Hap's turn and he had decided to do the Great Hoover Sweep. Hap had gone to his local shopping centre one day and as he was walking through had noticed something happening on a stage.

'That gentleman over there, how about you, will you give it a go?' a voice bellowed over the loudspeaker.

Hap turned around, wondering who the spruiker was speaking to. He looked up and realised the gentleman was looking directly at him.

'Yes, you, how would you like to take on the challenger in this year's Great Hoover Sweep?'

Curious, Hap decided to find out what it was all about. Apparently it involved a race between a previous winner and a new challenger. The two would line up and, on the starting call, run to one side of the stage, pick up a load of washing, run back and put them into a washing machine, making sure to close the lid behind them. Then they had to race back, pick up a vacuum cleaner, hoover the carpet, race back again, take the clothes out of the washing machine, run over to the other side of the stage and put them into the drier, making sure to close the lid of the washing machine. Then they had to race over to the ironing board, put it up, race back, take the clothes out of the drier, put them in a basket, making sure to close the door of course, run over to the ironing board, iron a shirt, and then run over the finish line. The overall winner would take on the current Hoover Champion to decide who would wear the crown for a year and take home a swag of prizes, which included vacuum cleaners, washing machines and other household items.

Unable to resist, Hap took the challenge. He describes, highly animated, how he ran all over the stage, pushing and shoving, wiping the sweat from his brow. It's neck and neck; the contestants reach the final part of the race and Hap's female opponent is nudging ahead. Hap gives it all he has and slips in front at the finish. He now has the right to take on the next challenger.

Hap, if he chooses, must come back in one hour to defend his win because at the end of the day, the person left will challenge the Hoover Champion to become the Overall Hoover Champion of Australia.

The pressure was on. Hap went home, changed out of his suit and got into some serious gear. Tracksuit and runners. He was back in an hour to take on any new challengers. He spent the entire day challenging anyone who dared, leaving a trail of victims behind him.

Then, finally, he was up against the reigning champion. Betty the Bruiser. A powerful, threatening figure, someone who obviously had washed a few shirts in her time, someone who knew how to iron a shirt or two! The clock went, the race was on. They raced all over the stage. Betty was in front, Hap just couldn't match her pace. This woman was taking no prisoners. They were approaching the final part of the race, Hap was pushing to catch her, sweat dripping from his brow. There was only one way he could win and he knew it! The ironing board.

Hal raced to the board to find Betty in the process of putting hers up. Hap picked up his board and, using a technique he had mastered over years of trying to finish his ironing as quickly as possible, grabbed it at an angle close to his body and snapped it open. That was the crucial moment. He took the lead. But Betty was pretty handy with an iron and now it was neck and neck again. They finished at the same time and raced to the line. Hap threw himself across the finish, millimetres ahead of Betty. He had won!

The crowd cheered. Hap was the new Overall Hoover Champion of Australia.

To hear Hap tell the story was hilarious. He had the whole room in hysterics. Not bad for a speech that was ad lib.

It was obvious that Hap would win, but I was surprised and delighted to come runner-up. This meant that both Hap and I would contest the next stage, the area competition, to be held in two weeks' time.

With the opportunity to prepare and add more than a little colour, Hap's speech got better and better. He went on to win each level of competition until he finally won the Australian championships. By that time his speech was so funny, he had everyone rolling in the aisles. He finished the speech by telling the audience that he had renamed Betty the Bruiser, Amiable Alice, and she now did his cleaning for him!

By the time the international competition came around we all had more experience and once again I volunteered. Everyone said that I should talk about my accident, and how I overcame so many challenges. It was an obvious choice, I agreed, but how on earth was I to tell the story in five to seven minutes? I would have to leave so much out.

I did the best I could and came up with what I thought was a pretty good speech. On the night of the competition Hap and I reversed positions from the humorous speech— I came first and Hap was runner-up. Actually, Hap was such a good speaker I think he had become a bit blasé about winning—he just assumed he would. I snuck up and surprised him!

I went on to win the next level and then reached the final stage before the trip to the States. I gave what I felt was a good speech that night, and when it was over everyone thought I would take home the honours.

As it turned out I didn't win but came second. Although disappointed at first, I soon discovered that this was actually the best thing that could have happened to me. It gave me the opportunity to start something bigger in my life, something that would change my life beyond my expectations.

I was about to embark on a whole new journey.

Chapter 7

'JANINE, YOU HAVE to write a book about this!'

As soon as I arrived home from hospital, my friends began telling me I should write about what I had been through. At the time it was the last thing on my mind. My only thought was to learn to walk again, and to get some level of independence back.

One of my friends offered to lend me a computer and although I appreciated the thought I was in no state to write about anything. I couldn't sit down for any length of time because the plaster cast covering my body was too restricting. I was tired all the time as my body was recovering from major and multiple trauma. I could hardly think, let alone put my thoughts on paper.

Not only that, I had a lot of learning to do. When someone goes through an accident of some sort, it is almost as though they go through a metamorphosis. They become a new person, inside and out. The person I was before my accident was dead, and I had to discover the new me, to go out and find a new direction for my life. I had a lot of searching to do before I could even consider putting anything on paper.

However, ever since Toastmasters had ended, for a while anyway, I had been feeling restless. I knew the time to write had finally come.

'I'm ready to write my book,' I said to Tim one night soon after the competition.

'That's great, honey,' Tim said.

'I really feel that coming second was a blessing in disguise. I'm ready to write my book and if I had won I wouldn't have had the time. Now I can put all my energies into writing.'

One reason for wanting to write was to help anyone else who was facing a similar fate. I knew if I had had something similar to read after my accident it would have helped immensely. I also knew it was another step in my recovery, and would be a great catharsis for me.

I knew I had made a remarkable recovery, my doctors attested to that. But I also knew that as far as I had come, I still had a way to go. It wasn't in my best interests to push the accident aside; after all, it was because of the accident that I had become the person that I was. Remembering the events and the trauma, however difficult, was part of the recovery and I wanted to feel proud of what I had been through.

I had grieved and cried; I had plunged to the depths of depression and clawed my way back to forge a life I considered every bit as fulfilling as the one I had before, in fact even more so. I knew about disappointments and I knew about heartache. I knew what it meant to lose everything, not just physically, but to lose one's very self, to lose one's dignity.

But one thing I didn't know was how to type! There are those who say real writers write longhand, but I had neither the patience nor the time to do that. I would just have to learn to type.

For a long time Tim and I had been discussing the possibility of buying a computer. I was still allowed a student's discount. So, after hunting around for the best price, we purchased a reasonable computer and printer. My first trip into a computer software store was like discovering a lolly shop for the first time. I couldn't believe my eyes. There were so many games! Needless to say, when I came home from my shopping expedition, Tim was a little cross.

'How can we afford all that?' was his remark.

'Don't worry, I put it on my credit card, I'll pay for them all later.'

I knew I had got carried away, but I wasn't about to let a small thing like money detract from my enjoyment. I had come home with golf games, flying simulators, children's games—educational of course—and quite a few other interesting programs, as well as my typing tutorial. When Tim saw how much fun it all was, he soon forgot about my indulgence.

We had a lot of fun with the games, especially the flying ones; we would set up the fighter jet and have dogfights, but most of all we used to love flying into the trees and through the hangar. It became a competition between us as to who could get through with the greatest degree of accuracy.

I started my typing course, which guaranteed to teach me how to type in just ten lessons. There were two parts to the program, one to build accuracy and one to increase speed. When I was working on the speed program, if I took too long hitting the next key, the computer would beep at me. One night I was downstairs practising my typing, when instead of hearing the little beep, the strangest thing happened. The computer said, 'Hurry up now, get a move on!'

I sat there absolutely shocked. It was the strangest little voice. I started to type again and lo and behold the voice spoke again. I was flabbergasted—the computer had taken on a life of its own.

This happened for a while, and each time I felt a little more uneasy, then all of a sudden I heard Tim laughing. He had been watching me for some time. The joke was that he had been playing around and had discovered how to replace the beep with a personalised message. It was his voice, unrecognisable of course, coming out of the computer.

Tim was fast becoming computer literate and this wasn't the last joke he was to play on me. However, I too soon learnt how to use the sound and left a few of my own messages for him to discover.

After I had been typing for a few weeks, I noticed that my right arm was beginning to ache. I went to my local doctor to try to ascertain what the cause was. My right arm had been broken in the accident, one of the many bones broken. It had become quite disfigured in fact, with a very large lump over the area that had been broken. It always hurt to a degree but I had become immune to the pain—I had so many parts that ached this was just another. I had been examined from top to bottom—literally—as part of the procedure for my court case, so my arm had been looked over extensively. However, now it was beginning to bother me.

'Do you think it might be a stress fracture?' I asked my doctor.

'No, very unlikely. It's probably just strained. I want you to try and rest it,' she said.

That was all well and good but when you have a small

baby, it is almost impossible to rest your arm completely. I stopped typing; I didn't have much choice, it hurt too much. My arm got worse, until finally I could no longer pick up a tea cup.

I returned to my doctor for the third time and she agreed I should have it x-rayed. After the procedure I returned home with the photos. They are always sealed so the doctor can open them but I like to have a sneak preview.

'Listen to this, Tim, it says that I have a nonunion of the distal part of the ulna, consistent with previous fracture. That sounds to me like I have a broken arm.'

How could this possibly be true? My arm had been treated in hospital and I had been sent home with it supposedly healed. It couldn't be broken.

I took out the X-ray and held it up to the light. My arm was broken all right. I could see light shining right through the bones.

I was shocked to say the least.

Straightaway I phoned Doctor Stephen and I told him what the report said. He confirmed my diagnosis: six and a half years after my accident, my right arm was still broken. Everything I had done, all the flying, I had done with a broken arm. I knew I had a high pain threshold, but this was ridiculous!

'You'd better come in and see me, we'll need to operate,' Doctor Stephen said.

It was really out of Doctor Stephen's area—he looked after my back, not my arm—but he was the only one I would trust to operate on me. He told me that he would have to insert a plate in my arm to give it a chance of uniting again. I would then be required to have my arm in plaster for six weeks.

I was booked into the Mater Hospital the week before Christmas. I had been to quite a few hospitals in Sydney but this was my first visit to the Mater. Everyone kept telling me what a wonderful place it was, but as far as I was concerned I had spent more than enough time in hospitals already.

Before long I was in familiar territory, sitting in pre-op, ready for Doctor Stephen.

'Hello, Janine, how are you?' Doctor Stephen said as he leaned over my trolley bed.

'Don't you get the arm mixed up this time,' I replied. 'It's the right one.' This had become a joke between us, and he always feigned ignorance.

I was wheeled into the theatre and before long that familiar needle was in my arm again. I hated this part. The feeling of coldness creeping up my arm and down my body, my eyes starting to close. It is such a loss of control that I will never be able to accept it.

When I woke up, my arm was hurting badly. This was supposed to be a minor operation as far as I was concerned, and I thought I would be in and out of hospital in one day. It certainly wasn't meant to hurt this much.

I later learned that it had taken a fair bit of pushing and shoving to repair my arm. Doctor Stephen had first to expose the fracture site, then to chew away at all the fibrous tissue that had built up. Next he had to align the two pieces of broken bone until the two ends were joined, and hold them together with a clamp. The clamp held the arm in place while they drilled holes into the bone and inserted the screws. I should have learnt by now that anything connected to orthopaedics involves a lot of pain.

I looked down at my arm and it was wrapped up as though it had been mummified. Green bandages everywhere, and plaster under there somewhere. I had falsely believed that a few days after the operation I would be able to start typing again. It was fast looking as though I would have to re-evaluate the situation.

I had to stay in hospital overnight. Mum called to see how I was but I was too groggy from the anaesthetic to talk. I invariably get sick from it and vomit for hours afterwards, and this time was no exception. Mum was looking after Annabel while I was in hospital as Tim was flying, and I preferred that she didn't bring her in to see me. There are too many bugs in hospitals that babies are susceptible to.

Early the next day, still feeling sick, I decided I was ready to go home.

'How do you feel today, Janine, still nauseous?' the nurse asked.

'No, I feel great,' I lied, desperate to go home.

The nurse had to help me pack up my things and she wheeled me out to the foyer in a wheelchair. Mum couldn't come and pick me up because Annabel was asleep, and Tim was working, so I had to catch a taxi.

I probably looked rather silly. I mean, how often do you see patients catching a taxi home from hospital by themselves? I must have looked like an escapee.

Because I wasn't in hospital, I wouldn't be able to have any pethidine, so they had sent me home with the strongest painkillers available in tablet form. It was like putting a bandaid on a broken limb. But I only had myself to blame: I really should have stayed a few more nights, but I was too proud and stubborn to admit it.

I had a frustrating Christmas. It was boiling hot and I was unable to swim, and when I can't do anything I am like a bear with a sore head. I couldn't type either, which drove me mad because I was raring to go with my book. The one thing I could do was read, however, and I went through a lot of books over that Christmas, jotting down ideas with my left arm as I went. I wondered whether I would have enough material to fill a book, but as I sat and waited, the passion to write started to build and I knew I had to give it a go.

In a way, having to go back into hospital to have another operation was like reliving the accident all over, which I knew was what I would have to do to write my book successfully. In that sense it was good preparation for me.

I remember, after the operation, standing at the kitchen sink and talking to Tim.

'You know, I still find it hard to believe that this has happened so far down the track. Why do these things always happen to me?' I asked rhetorically.

Tim looked at me and in his typical Irish manner replied, 'Oh well, at least it's another chapter!'

Chapter 8

PRIOR TO MY OPERATION I had begun approaching publishing houses to gauge interest in my story. If no-one took my book on, I had already decided that I would publish it myself. Although I was writing primarily because I saw it as a major part of my recovery process, I also wanted to leave something permanent for Annabel to read when she was older so she would understand why her mummy was different.

I rang at least ten publishing houses in one day and got more or less the same response each time: send in a synopsis and we'll get back to you.

I scratched out a few pages and decided to test them out on some friends to see if they were worth reading.

My closest girlfriends were ideal for the task, at least they would be honest. We all met up for dinner one night and I hesitantly asked them if they would mind listening to what I had written.

I sat down and began reading. There was absolute silence and I was sure they were hating it.

Reaching the end, I looked up to see if I could anticipate their response.

'That was great, Nino. I can't wait to read the rest,' Erica said, and the others all agreed. I breathed a huge sigh of relief. I had passed the first test.

I ran off a few copies and sent them to the various publishing houses. Not too long afterwards I received my first rejection. Then they came flooding in. As polite as they all were, I figured that they were probably standard letters from people who may not have even read my sypnosis. Anyway, I wasn't going to let that stop me! I wondered how long I would have to wait before I got some positive feedback. Then I received two letters, both from Christian publishing houses, which were positive and helpful and gave me something to hope for. I was extremely encouraged and although they didn't promise anything firm, I felt that at least my story had been carefully considered.

Unsure of which publishing house would do the best job, I thought I would put something more concrete together and then weigh up any offers I might get. But I didn't want to jump ahead of myself—maybe I wouldn't get any offers at all.

I was plagued by the niggling doubt that I had only written ten pages and writing an entire book was something completely different. It was a daunting challenge. But I wasn't about to let self-doubt stop me now. If I didn't have a go I would never know.

The six weeks seemed more like six years but finally the cast was removed and I had a new arm, extremely emaciated but at least it wasn't broken anymore. There was some chance I would have to go back in a year's time to have the plate removed as it would weaken the bone if it remained in my arm. But that was the furthest thing from my mind because I could at last begin writing.

There was only one problem—I didn't know where to start. Where was the beginning? I had been giving it much thought, but didn't seem to be making any progress. I had sat down a few times at the computer and tried to find some inspiration, but none came. In retrospect, I realise I was trying too hard to adopt an acceptable literary style, but it just wasn't me.

Giving it some thought in bed one morning, I remembered some advice I had been given—be honest, accurate and just tell it how it was. Be down to earth. I suddenly realised that all I had to do was simply tell my story.

I leapt out of bed and hurried downstairs to my computer. I was filled with excitement as I started typing.

'Gasping for breath, I reached for the oxygen mask that was covering my face. Something, or someone, stopped my attempt to free myself from it. I couldn't see anything even though my eyes were open, but I could feel the pressure of the grip that now had my wrist in a tight lock.'

I knew this was right; it felt right.

'A tube in my mouth reached down to my stomach and made me feel nauseous. Slowly, I lifted my hands and blinked to clear my vision. I could see that they were attached to a series of tubes that prevented me from moving them any distance.'

I had to begin with the accident; after all, that was the beginning of this story.

I could recall exactly what it felt like to wake up in hospital. One minute I was riding a bike with my friends, the next I was in a hospital bed. I was confused, my body consumed by pain. As I wrote, I relived the feelings as though they were happening then and there.

I had thrown my readers smack bam in the middle of my trauma, but that was how it was for me. That was the most honest place to begin.

I continued to write that day, and the next and the next. It just seemed to flow. I wrote until I had twenty typed pages. Then, as at least six months had passed since I had received replies back from publishing houses, I decided to try a few more.

In conversation with the owner of our local bookshop, Phillip Bray, one day, I mentioned I was going to write a book about my experience. I think I actually liked telling people because then I felt I was committed to starting, as if I had put myself on the line.

Phillip suggested I try Pan Macmillan publishers who had recently published *Cry of the Damaged Man*, a book written by a doctor who had been in an accident. That showed that they were at least interested in that kind of story.

When I got home I called them and with a little wrangling, arranged a meeting for Wednesday. Having had some very positive feedback from Sally Millner Publishing, I was confident enough to ask for an interview rather than simply send my stuff in and wait and see. I am a great believer in being able to sell oneself in the flesh.

Wednesday arrived and I was up early. I had put together a folder of newspaper clippings and anything else I thought might help, even a few recordings of radio interviews I had given in the past. I packed up everything into a briefcase and set off for Pan Macmillan.

Upon arrival, I was ushered upstairs to meet with Jane, the acquisitions editor. We walked up a few flights of steep stairs before entering a large area with offices on each side. My first impression was how messy it was—there were books and paper all over the place. Everything seemed very squashed.

Jane took me into her boss's office so we would have some room to talk. It was wall to wall books. There were books filling the bookcase, books on the desks, books on the coffee table and many piles of manuscripts. In fact I had to move a few books off the lounge to sit down! They obviously did a lot of reading in this place.

I immediately felt at ease with Jane. We were roughly the same age and we just clicked. Before I got out my pages, she asked me to tell her about the accident. I started to tell her my history, from an early age as an athlete, to my lead-up to selection for the Olympics and then the accident. I talked about my depression and about how I had got into flying. In fact, I talked and talked and talked. Jane just sat there and listened. When I finished she said, 'Well, that's a great story. I'm sure we would be interested in publishing it.'

I was taken aback. She hadn't even read what I had written; she might hate it. I tried to warn her about my writing abilities, that I had never written anything before, had no formal training, so it might be an absolute mess.

'I can tell by the way you talk about the accident, that you can write,' Jane assured me.

I left her my draft and she promised to call by Friday. I looked at my watch; I had been with her for one and a half hours. The time had passed so quickly, I must have done quite a bit of talking!

Jane had explained that it was necessary for her to discuss the project with James, the publishing director, and that the decision wasn't his alone, but had to be approved by a committee of people. If everyone liked my proposal then they would make me an offer for publication. I had no idea what Jane would think when she read my few pages, written by an absolute novice as they were. I would just have to wait till Friday to find out.

The next morning I was downstairs in the office when the phone rang. I was more than a little surprised when I learnt it was Jane. It wasn't Friday yet.

But that was nothing compared to my surprise when she told me she had read my draft last night and hadn't been able to put it down. She wanted to meet me next week with James to discuss a contract.

Barely able to speak with excitement I agreed to meet them the following Monday in a coffee shop in Balmain. I was over the moon. Just imagine that. A big publishing house was ready to make me an offer!

The rest of the week seemed to drag and when Monday finally arrived I was early for the meeting. I am one of those people who is always early, even when I'm not half as excited as I was that day.

After the introductions were out of the way James said they were very keen to publish my book. He said they believed it would be a bestseller and they intended to print first in hardcover then follow up later in soft.

I didn't want to sound too keen—there was still a lot of negotiating to do—and I didn't want to sound too naive. I told him that I was unsure of which way to go, that I had approached a few publishers who had expressed interest.

'Janine,' James said, 'I don't want to sound pushy, but we will do a great job with your book. We are looking at doing a similar job to the one we have done with Sara Henderson's book.'

I had read *From Strength to Strength* and knew that it had sold extremely well. If they could do a similar job for me then I would be very impressed. I was well aware that no matter how well a book is written or how good the story is, success really comes down to marketing. A publisher can make or break a book.

Finally, without making any firm indication as to which

way I would go, I left them, James saying he would put together an offer and ring me the next day.

James did as he promised and offered me an advance of money to write. I told him I needed to think it over and would ring in a few days. I was still in shock; I couldn't believe I was really talking business with a publisher. Everything seemed to be happening so quickly. I needed some advice.

I did some ringing around and discovered a wonderful organisation called the Society of Authors which gives advice to budding writers regarding all sorts of things. I joined up and spoke at length to their legal department. I wanted to know what I should be looking for in a contract and what I should be asking for. I had decided that I wanted to negotiate the contract on my own, rather than through an agent, so that I could stay in touch with what was happening. They sent me a booklet outlining a standard contract and then I went over the changes I wanted made.

A week later I rang James and told him that I would accept his offer of an advance but that I had a few requests regarding my contract. He seemed pleased with that and we made an appointment to get together to discuss it. I guess I had a nerve walking into his office and demanding changes. After all, I was hardly a successful writer who was in demand. Quite the contrary—I was a complete unknown. Despite this, I felt I had just as much to offer them as they did me.

Surprisingly, he agreed to almost all of my requests and shortly after we shook hands and I left his office with a firm offer and a contract that I was more than happy with.

I was now part of a team and was committed to writing a book. I didn't know it then, but I was off and running on an adventure that would turn my life upside down.

C*hapter* 9

MY WRITING BEGAN in earnest.

According to my contract, I had until November to finish the book. That gave me only six months. That was not a whole lot of time considering I had a young daughter to look after. Actually, James had initially asked me if I thought I could have it finished in two months so they could get it out for Christmas!

I soon discovered, however, that putting pen to paper—figuratively speaking, of course—was going to be the easy part: I had underestimated how tough it would be to relive the entire accident, every minute detail of it. I was going to have to go back and remember things that I had hidden away in my memory. This was going to be a very big lesson in self-development, but I was only to discover that some way down the track.

Trying to sequence the events had me stumped for a while. Eventually I decided that the best way was to write everything down on paper, all the events that I could remember, and then try to piece them together in some sort of pattern.

Another challenge was trying to remember all the medical terminology. I had a good recollection of the medical procedures I was put through but I needed someone to make sure that I had all the jargon correct. Adrian was just the person.

When I left hospital I had been given a discharge summary of my stay. I dug up these notes along with a few other things that would come in handy. Mum had kept a diary of my stay in hospital and she brought it over to me. As I flicked through it I felt overwhelmingly sad at what she and Dad must have endured. Something I could only now fully appreciate having become a mother myself.

I had received stacks of mail in hospital, a lot of it from strangers who, having read about my accident, wanted to send me their good wishes. It had been years since I had read these letters and cards. There had been so many of them pinned up on the wall behind my hospital bed that the nurses used to laugh that I was a fire hazard. Mum had packed them all up and, although I hadn't looked at them since, I had never thrown them out, I just couldn't bear to. They had meant everything to me; they had kept me going and I needed them to be kept safely even if I never looked at them again.

I tipped the pile out on the floor and began. As I read I released just how important my family and friends were in my recovery process. Many of the letters made me stop and thank God for the goodness of people, for so many of them were from people I didn't know.

Dear Janine
Just a short note to let you know that my thoughts are with you.
I have always admired your tremendous drive and determination
and know that these qualities will help you through this tough
time.

Dear Janine

You don't know me but I guess you are receiving a lot of fan mail. What a wonderful girl you are and an inspiration to so many people. I know you will be back on your feet and in that cross-country skiing competition in no time. You have the will to do it.

My son has gone to the Commowealth Games for judo and I was so worried because he had a hamstring injury when he left here. When I saw you on TV today I realised how stupid I was, when you have so many injuries to cope with now.

We will be watching your progress ... All the best to you and your family who are helping you cope.

Keep your chin up, you're a great gal!

Dear Janine

I am a complete stranger to you so I hope you understand why I'm writing. Your interview was on Channel Nine this morning and I wish to pass on to you my sympathy and I pray for a quick recovery.

You are about the same age as my granddaughters whom I love dearly. I know how I should feel if the same thing happened to one of them ...

You nearly made it to my lovely town of Leura and I hope that one day you get here. We would welcome you.

Bless you Janine for your courage and cheerful smile. God be with you always.

Dear Janine

... Aren't you a wonderful positive lady. I felt very sad hearing of your tragic accident.

But you are doing your best, even now, being positive.

You will make it Janine, with your strong mind and heart and happy voice. You can! The strength you get from your family, friends and medical team will help you to get there.

I'm writing to let you know that my thoughts and prayers are with you.

Dear Janine

You probably don't remember me in the least, but I am that American guy who attended your aerobic classes at Macquarie University. I've been meaning to write to wish you the speediest of a full recovery. When I read in the paper about your accident I just had a feeling deep down inside that you'd 'be back' in full swing after a period of rehabilitation. Really! Even though I hardly know you, you gave me a feeling that you are not only a 'fighter' but that you are a 'survivor' in the truest sense of the word.

I have a feeling that you're the sort of person who, if they say will 'walk' again, you will say, 'No, I'm not only going to do that, but anything else I decide to do', in other words, you will progress far above and beyond what 'they' say you can do, largely because you were so healthy beforehand, combined with your 'persevering' and 'positive' mental outlook. It will be difficult but if anyone can fully recover it will be you.

Anyway, I just wanted to let you know that people you have no idea of are pulling for you and wishing you the best in your 'fight'. Your smile and positive vibes have left good impressions on many people and I'm sure they will continue to do so once you get out of hospital again. You have a lot to offer as a person.

Then I read a letter from one of my good friends, Bob.

Thought it time to write a little letter and let you know how much I am thinking of you. Well, today is the day of your big operation. I spoke to the sister in intensive care and she said things went well. During my lunchtime as I ran through the Sydney Harbour National Park, I thought constantly of you and the accident, wondering why, why, why? Isn't it the sort of thing that happens to someone else? When such a thing happens, all your close friends are greatly affected. Every day, whether it be at the office, driving to work or lying in bed late at night, I often start thinking of you, the past and the future.

Ever since we met during our early days at university I've seen

Janine Shepherd tackle and defeat many demanding physical challenges. She has set her goals at the highest level, made a commitment to achieve these and done so.

Well, your biggest challenge is ahead of you now and by far the toughest. At times the physical and mental strain will be like nothing else but as in the past . . . you will win.

The times ahead will not be easy but remember you have a group of close friends who will be there all the time. To date your powers of recovery have amazed everyone. In the future, you will not only surprise us all, but yourself, wait and see!

So remember when you are there on your own thinking hard, lots of people love you very much and want you back.

Remember the fun times we had together like the photo on the front of this card. It won't be long before the Janine I know is around again.

I barely made it to the end of the letter before the tears began rolling down my face. I turned the page to see the photo Bob had photocopied. It showed a group of us sitting on a rock at the snow. It was from a university ski trip when we all went down to select the team for the upcoming intervarsity competition.

We all had huge smiles on our faces, it was such a great time we were having.

I wiped the tears from my face and as I looked at the photo I remembered what it was like to be able to ski, to run, to have a body that did what it was meant to do. I didn't have that anymore.

I cried because those times were over. I had changed so much since the accident; I had been forced to in order to survive. I felt it was a great loss that I was no longer a part of that circle of friends because I wasn't involved in sport. They had wanted me to stay a part of them so much, and I appreciated that, but it was just too painful. Like putting salt on the wound.

I remember one night, not long after I had been released from hospital, some of my friends took me out to dinner. They started to talk about an upcoming triathlon and some new bike gear they had purchased. They thought nothing of talking like that—training was always the dominant topic of conversation around my group of friends. But for me it hurt too much to be reminded of what I had lost.

I regretted that I had shut my friends out. I had been so intent on putting on a brave face that I was afraid to tell them how depressed I really was. I should have trusted them more and shared more.

I fumbled through some more mail. I came across a letter from the Department of Sport and Recreation saying how sorry they were to learn of my accident and the extensive injuries I had suffered. They wished me the speediest of recoveries on behalf of all those associated in sport in New South Wales.

There was a letter from the then Minister for Sport and Recreation and Minister for Tourism, Michael Cleary:

I was most upset when I heard of your recent serious accident. I hope that you will recover from your injuries as soon as possible.

I am sure your tremendous competitive spirit which you displayed in sport will assist you greatly at this time.

There were letters from people I hadn't seen in years, people I had lost contact with. There were even letters from people I had gone to primary school with. I came across a lovely letter from the coach of the Canadian ski team, Marty Hall, and felt again the keen disappointment at having missed out on the opportunity to train with him. It had been the ultimate compliment to be invited to join the Canadian team in preparation for the Olympics, and perhaps Marty was right when he said, 'Janine, I believe you can make it, but not if you stay in Australia.'

Unfortunately, this country just doesn't have the resources or facilities to support our winter sports athletes. I have always believed, however, that despite this Australia could achieve success in winter sports. It shouldn't come as a surprise to know that I believe wholeheartedly that if you want something badly enough and you're willing to work hard, then anything is possible.

When I found a poem that my friend Pab had written for me I laughed. It was so silly that I had stuck it up on the mirror above my head. That way every time I looked up at it, it reminded me not to take things so seriously. The poem is called 'Grovelling.'

The Janine Machine is looking green
She's strapped from head to toe it seems
But still her eyes do brightly gleam
And keep alive the burning dream.
Anything you do will mean what you do to it do meaning give
And life without a dreaming soul is hardly worth the while to live.
For who cares that we won IV
It only matters to you and me
Unless you try there's nothing you see
You're lost in endless apathy
But with a dream that carries on
Not always straight but always along
It helps to fight what may go wrong
A sad verse in a ballad song.
Janine has fought and will fight more.
With cutting pain her back is sore
We can help with all the chores
For her the burden is much more.
She must cope and hope must be
That she will again walk normally
And in her bed she must lie straight

What a bloody grovelling fate!
We cannot question why or when
Or how the diver got the bends
We'll see it through until the end
On that you can surely depend
The Janine Machine is always keen
To plan ahead and always scheme
And soon she will again be mean
And again pursue the unending dream.

Pab may not have been the world's best poet, but his heart was in the right place!

I had to laugh later when he came over to visit me at home. When I told him I was writing a book he came out with a classic Pab comment.

'If I'd known you were writing a book, I would have come to visit you more often in hospital.'

I was deeply affected by all the letters and cards. I felt so grateful that I had had such support to sustain me throughout my ordeal. I couldn't have done it without such a wonderful group of friends and well-wishers. I felt so loved; I don't think I had ever felt that as strongly as I did right now. It is amazing how it often takes a tragedy to bring out the best in people, and I had seen the very best.

I had kept in contact with the crew at the rescue helicopter base and I asked them to send me a copy of my transfer documents from the accident. Whenever I was out at Prince Henry Hospital I visited the base and one day they offered to take me for a ride.

I accepted of course, but felt anxious as I glanced over the helicopter before getting in. I had never really looked inside the chopper that had played such a major part in my life.

Paul had been the crewman on duty the night of my accident, so there was a certain bond between us. He filled me in on many of the details of the accident and the subsequent procedures. Apparently, when the call came, they were told the pick-up was a VIP. This meant the press would be informed of the accident details, which was how the newspapers had got onto my story so quickly.

Paul showed me around the helicopter and I saw the spot where the stretcher was placed. It was an eerie feeling. I imagined what I must have looked like lying there that night. Of course I remembered nothing, but for Paul the picture would stay in his mind forever.

The chopper ride turned out to be fun; we flew all over Sydney and along the beaches and then back to the hospital base. While I was in the office the crew dug up the records of the job and gave me a copy.

I also decided to apply for my hospital records and, after filling out a few forms, a huge bundle of notes arrived in the mail. I read each page with an enormous sense of disbelief. Could this really have happened to me? I could barely comprehend that my body had been subjected to so much trauma.

It is a miracle that I ever survived.

I tried to make some sense of the scribbled doctors' notes, wondering that anyone could decipher them. The night of my accident: 'Confused, rambling response, unreliable response to neurological exam'. I obviously had no idea of how I came to be in hospital. 'Main problem at present hypotension and abdominal trauma.'

Then hypovolamic shock, in ward one. 'Unpalpable BP. Clinically shocked, pale sweaty, tachycardia . . . ' The list of symptoms went on and on.

'Continues to indicate further blood loss, has abdominal signs and fever.' There were very sketchy diagrams of my abdominal area and back with shading to show the areas of trauma. There was severe bruising and blistering around the entire abdomen.

I read some more. 'Distressed with pain in back. Morphine infusion commenced.' I remembered how it felt to be lying there on my back with so many broken bones and so much swelling and bruising. The pain was intolerable and there was no escape from it.

'Did not sleep at all overnight, continually talking, asking when she will be turned, and for more ice.' I remember begging to be turned, the momentary relief when the pressure was taken off my back. The cool sensation of ice in my mouth had become a craving. I remember it was Uncle Darryl who had given me the ice.

'Needs a lot of reassurance and explanation. Visited by family.' I was scared, unsure of what was happening. 'Very uncomfortable night. Analgesia not holding the pain.' There were so many comments, most of them saying the same thing—pain, inability to sleep, distressed state.

The memories of the spinal unit were suddenly so fresh in my mind. Strangely, the indignities were almost harder to forget than the pain. Spinal patients are subjected to the most humiliating tests. As necessary as they might be, they are still abhorrent and occasionally made no easier by some of the medical staff associated with the specialty. I remember having to go through a series of tests called urodynamics to assess the level of damage to my bladder and other internal organs.

It is the most undignified process that one could ever imagine. I had had one before I left the hospital, and because I was still a patient it was just tolerable. However, when I had left the hospital I was required to return for another test at a later date.

Daven had driven me to the hospital for the test.

As I entered the room and was placed on the bed,

wearing only a hospital gown which doesn't hide very much, I noticed that there were quite a few people present. In fact there must have been at least six in the room.

I had to lie down and have a catheter inserted and my bladder was then filled. While I was having this humiliating procedure performed on me, the strangers stood by and watched. I was too embarrassed to speak up and to ask them to leave.

The doctor stood by and talked to them through the procedure, referring to me as if I were a dummy, there to be spoken about and not to. They were all looking attentively at what I was being subjected to, oblivious to the fact I was shrinking with shame.

After the test was over, the doctor spoke to me for the first time.

'We'll be in contact with the results. You can put your clothes back on now.' And that was all he said.

Humiliated, I just smiled nervously and then called Daven in to help me get out to the car. But it had all been too much for me. As soon as I saw him, I burst into tears.

Later, when I had calmed down, I decided to write to the doctor involved and tell him exactly what I thought of his inconsiderate treatment. I was astounded when I received his reply. He said he was sorry that I felt that way, but it was a training hospital so therefore it was necessary for student doctors to be present.

How arrogant! He didn't even have the common courtesy to at least get my permission before he let the doctors in. I was too embarrassed and surprised to speak up at the time, but I was certain that I would never again go for one of those tests.

That was only one occasion; there were many more incidents that were just as humiliating. Being in hospital is tough enough, why on earth do some uncompassionate individuals have to make it so much harder? Perhaps if only the roles could be reversed, these people would learn to be a little more understanding.

Chapter 10

MONTHS PASSED AND all my spare time was taken up with writing. My only free full day was every second Wednesday when Mum looked after Annabel. Every other week she looked after her other granddaughter. Mum would also come and give me a break whenever she could; however, it was difficult to get into a rhythm when I only had one or two hours free.

I found I needed at least an hour to stop thinking about other things and get into the right frame of mind to write. When Tim was home from work, I would race off and grab whatever time I could to sit down and type. Even though we attempted to keep Annabel out of the office, she was forever coming into the room to see what Mummy was doing.

She must have formed an opinion at a very young age that all Mummy did was sit at the computer and write books! I spent a lot of time typing with her on my lap. I would be deep in thought and typing frantically when she would interrupt. Rather than stop mid-sentence I would keep writing until she made it quite clear that she wanted me to stop.

One of the advantages of all this was that Annabel became computer literate at a very young age. She would sit at the computer and play all sorts of games which she just loved. Sometimes, however, this proved quite a problem. Occasionally I would have to leave the terminal for a short time and then, unbeknownst to me, Annabel would sneak into the room to see what delights she could discover there. One day her inquisitiveness got the better of her and when I returned to the screen I was horrified. The whole text had been scrambled. All I could see was a series of hieroglyphics; I just prayed I had remembered to save what I had last written because, if I hadn't, there was no hope of my remembering it. As it turned out, the problem was easily rectified but for a moment it gave me quite a scare.

But I wouldn't have had it any other way. I wanted Annabel with me and if that meant things were slightly more complicated then so be it. I didn't want to put her in day care. I know I was overprotective, which was partly related to my accident and was something I struggled with, but for now I wanted her to be with me.

Besides, Annabel had had a rough time since her birth. She was often sick; not with any major illness, just with a continual series of niggling infections which we were told were common to all babies.

While we were living in Tamworth we had taken her to a doctor who always prescribed antibiotics for her. I began to suspect her judgement and never felt completely confident with her. On one occasion she prescribed yet another course of antibiotics for yet another bacterial infection. Annabel had developed a rash over her face that worried me. It was only when we returned to Sydney that we discovered she had in fact had quite a bad case of staph infection.

Her minor illnesses carried on for a year; then one day she developed a raging fever which wasn't relieved with Panadol. Unable to reduce the fever, Tim and I took her up to the local hospital. By this stage she was in a fairly distressed state. The doctors took a urine sample and immediately I knew things weren't good. I had had enough of my own to know a urinary tract infection straightaway. And for a baby to have a UTI there had to be something wrong.

We were sent to a paediatric urologist to discuss the results. He sent us for a series of routine tests which were traumatic for all of us. Annabel was only one. To see her, naked, struggling on the bare table as they inserted a catheter inside her tiny body hurt me terribly. She screamed as the hands pinning her down tightened their grip to keep her from moving. Maybe it would have been easier for me to have left the room, but she needed me there. I felt like a traitor, holding her down, trying to reassure her that it would soon be over.

At home, I rang my local doctor who said she would ring to find out the results of the test. She was unable to contact the urologist but instead got in contact with his registrar, who told her the results showed Annabel had ureteric reflux, and that she would almost certainly need surgery.

I was shattered. I had only known one other child with this condition—my cousin's son—and he had needed to have a kidney removed. I couldn't believe this was happening to my baby. My perfect little baby. I cried for her, wishing I could take her place. I had been through worse, I could handle it; but she couldn't, she was just a baby. This affected me far worse than any problem I had ever had.

For a week I tried to get used to the idea of Annabel needing surgery. It was too big an operation for such a little body. However, when we finally met with our urologist he told us that we had been misinformed by the registrar, that she wouldn't need surgery, not now at least, although she might in a year's time.

I was both relieved and outraged. How dare the registrar worry us so unnecessarily? He should have checked before racing ahead and giving us a false prognosis.

What Annabel needed was a course of antibiotics for one whole year. After that time she would be reassessed to see whether the reflux had improved. In actual fact, we were lucky that we had picked it up before her kidneys were damaged extensively. If after a year there was no improvement, then she would need surgery. So every day, for one year, we diligently followed a course of antibiotics to prevent any further infection.

I decided early on that I also wanted to discuss the condition with a naturopath. Because of my accident, I was open to anything that might assist the healing process. I was given the name of an excellent doctor, who was both a conventional GP and a naturopath. He had treated many children with ureteric reflux and had an excellent success rate. He examined Annabel and then prescribed a course of drops for her which he said would aid her development and the valves responsible for the reflux and help decrease the chances of her needing an operation.

Around the same time as we discovered the reflux, Annabel came down with a case of gastroenteritis, which for a small baby can be life-threatening. She had been vomiting all night and, not wanting to panic, Tim had tried to convince me that she would be all right if we kept up her fluids. But in the early morning she began to vomit green bile. Tim was flying that day so I had to take her to the hospital alone before the sun had even come up. She was so ill that as I struggled to carry her and myself into the hospital, her limp body dragged me down and made my task almost impossible.

She was immediately admitted to the ward and had to undergo several tests, which were not half as bad for her as they were for me. She was admitted to the isolation ward and put on a drip. I stayed with her for two days, sleeping—or trying to sleep—on an old chair beside her bed. She slowly came around then with the infusion of fluids in the drip and, finally, Tim came and took us home. We checked ourselves out of the hospital satisfied that Annabel was well on the road to recovery. Besides, Tim said if he left me there any longer I would be an absolute mess! With all the bugs and infections in hospitals, and my tendency to catch anything going, home seemed like the best place for both Annabel and myself.

The year passed and we finally returned for the tests to determine how Annabel was going. This time, thank goodness, the tests were less invasive and much less traumatic than the original series. With great trepidation, we waited for the results. As usual I opened them before reaching the doctor and even with my lack of medical training I understood that they indicated her reflux had corrected itself. I was ecstatic.

Whether or not the natural medicine had anything to do with it one will never know, but I prefer to think that it did.

Not long after I had begun writing, I went to a literary luncheon with my mum and Tim's mother. The three of us were making conversation with the other people sitting at the table, when I overheard Tim's mother talking about my book.

I was a little embarrassed; these people were strangers and I had a long long way to go before the book was ready.

'What sort of book is she writing?'

'Oh, it's an autobiography,' Marie said proudly.

'But she doesn't look old enough to write an auto-biography!' the lady said in a surprised voice.

'Well, it's about something that happened to her.' As Marie spoke the other lady listened attentively. 'And it has a real twist at the end.'

'Oh really? I'll make sure I get it. What's it called?'

Well, at least I would have one buyer, I thought.

I suppose I was bound to get some funny comments when people heard I was writing my autobiography; after all, no-one knew who I was. A typical conversation would go something like this:

'Do you work?'

'Oh well, yes, . . . I'm writing a book.'

'Oh really? What sort of book?'

A little self-consciously I would reply, 'Well, it's an auto-biography.'

To which the response invariably was, 'Oh really, who's it about?'

That one always got me!

At least by now I had thought up a title. Well, it had been Hap and I who had put our thinking caps on to come up with *Never Tell Me Never*. The reasoning behind it was simple. All the time people had been saying to me, You'll never do this or you'll never do that. I have never liked to be told that I could never do anything—in fact just hearing those words makes me more determined to prove them wrong.

Never Tell Me Never reflected precisely what my story was about, about never giving up, never accepting limits. Once I had a title, everything seemed to flow much easier.

Around this time I discovered I was going to have another baby. I was absolutely delighted. I had never for one moment imagined myself only having one child, which perhaps came partly from being one of three myself. I suppose I would have been excused if I hadn't had another, considering the problems I had with my body. But I have always been a glutton for punishment!

This pregnancy was going to be entirely different from the first. For a start my writing commitments weren't going to afford me a lot of time to exercise. With Annabel I had adopted the attitude that I was starting behind the eight ball. There had been doubt that I would even be able to conceive and when I had I was told I could expect all sorts of complications. I might have to spend large amounts of time in hospital, especially leading up to the birth, and I would need some sort of support for my back. I wouldn't be able to give birth vaginally due to the extent of injury to my back and because I had no pelvic tone to push the baby out.

Like everything I do, I took on my first pregnancy with great vigour. As far as I was concerned, it was an Olympic birth competition and I was in the running for a gold medal! I exercised, I swam, I lifted weights, I stretched. I watched my diet, determined to put on only the minimal amount of weight. I took every precaution I could to ensure my baby got the very best start in life, and that my body would stand up to the challenge.

Apart from an extremely painful birth—but then what birth isn't?—I had a normal vaginal delivery, much to my doctor's surprise. I had no anaesthetic, not because I wanted to be brave, but because it was contraindicated. Having an epidural always carries some risk, but for me the risk was far greater than it was for a woman with an undamaged back. I just had to put up with the pain or have a Caesarean, which I thought a bit dramatic if I was coping all right.

This second pregnancy wasn't going to be as easy, I knew that. I was a few years older, and my poor old body wasn't functioning quite as well as it had been. However, in what spare time I had, I did whatever exercise I could. I rode an exercise bike, which I find the epitome of boredom, but as I was unable to run it was the next best thing. I lifted a few light weights and did some stretching and watched my diet and weight gain. It would just have to do.

I even decided to give kayaking a go!

Tim and I had met a guy who lived nearby and ran sightseeing tours on the kayak. They had become very popular—what better way to see a harbour city? He invited us along one day and we jumped at the opportunity. Leg strength wasn't a prerequisite, and my arms were still very strong, so I was keen to give it a go.

I was only four months pregnant, so I thought nothing of going out on the harbour in a kayak. I didn't think we would be going very far, as it was our first time so I didn't think to take any supplies.

Patrick set Tim and I up in a tandem kayak and accompanied us in a single. We caught on pretty quickly and fell into a rhythm. It really was a lot of fun, so we headed off behind Patrick and before we knew it, the Harbour Bridge was looming over us! This spectacular sight was somewhat overshadowed by a huge tanker, which seemed to be coming straight towards us and we had to paddle quite frantically to get out of the way. With all the traffic on the harbour, we became very efficient at rapid paddling!

Patrick had told about this great little spot he knew on the other side of the bridge so we decided to head over to it. By this stage we were getting quite some distance from home and I had no idea how long it would take to get to this spot. We paddled for what seemed like hours and we still weren't there. I was getting pretty hungry by now and wished that I'd brought a bite to eat.

We finally made it to the beach and I was absolutely exhausted. If I didn't get some sugar into me right away I knew I would collapse. Patrick had to go up to the local shop and buy us some lollies and ice-creams which we devoured immediately. After all that paddling we had a quick rest and then headed back home!

Four hours after we started, we finally reached the shores where we'd began. Next time, I vowed, I wouldn't leave the house without a packed lunch!

Christmas approached and my first draft was due. I was running behind schedule but that didn't matter now because the publishing date had been pushed back to just before Christmas the following year, which seemed a long time away.

With the Christmas festivities taking everyone away from the office, it was into the new year before the edited manuscript was back to me. I was then told I had two weeks to go over it and make any final changes I wanted. Resembling a whale at this stage, I found it extremely uncomfortable to sit at a computer for any length of time, but I stuck to the deadline and said a final goodbye to my book. After this it was going to be near impossible to make any changes.

The entire experience of writing had been a revelation to me. Before I began, I believed I had coped well with my accident and thought I had recovered exceptionally well, not only on a physical level but also on an emotional one. However, when I began committing my thoughts to paper—or, more precisely, the screen—I discovered that I had so much more still to be resolved. There was so much pain inside me of which I had been unaware.

I would be sitting quietly, typing away, when suddenly I would begin to cry. Often I was not sure quite why, but somewhere in my heart there seemed to be some unexplained, unresolved hurt.

Tim would come in and wonder what on earth was happening.

'It's OK,' I would tell him, 'it's just hard to write about, that's all.'

I don't know if Tim could even begin to understand what I was going through; he hadn't known me when I had the accident, hadn't lived through it. Maybe it was unfair to expect him to understand.

Many times I wondered if it was worth torturing myself for. Perhaps it was for me to deal with alone. Why on earth would I want to share my innermost thoughts and most personal experiences with the world? Wasn't I setting myself up for more hurt when everyone read it?

In a strange way, I learnt more about myself through the writing process than I could ever have imagined. Even if no-one read the book, or even liked it, I knew it was bringing me one step further to a full recovery.

The next step was to go over my photos and try to make a selection for the book. As well as this we still had to get a cover shot. It had been arranged that I would meet a photographer at his studio one day, to have my make-up done and sit for a cover photograph.

I arrived and was swiftly seated to have my hair and make-up done. I was then taken outside for the photos. I had taken a few shirts so we took some shots in each of them. It all seemed such a rush. I have never been the sort of person to wear a lot of make-up, so to be madeup for the cover of my book just didn't seem natural to me.

I was right. When I saw the finished product, I knew they weren't right for the book. Although everyone at Pan loved them, it just wasn't me. We then went through a series of other photo sessions until I was feeling quite anxious that I couldn't get the right cover photo. And besides, time was running out in terms of print deadline—and I was about to have a baby!

I rang a good friend of mine, Tony, who is a photographer. I admitted that I wasn't really happy with the cover of the book.

'What about I come over today and take some shots and see how they turn out?'

It was already late morning and the sun was out in full force. We would be pushing it, but I agreed. We sat around that lunchtime—no make-up artist, no hair stylist—and as I sat on the chair on my front porch, Tony and I talked and joked as he took photo after photo. It was all a lot of fun. There were kids running around everywhere, but that didn't seem to matter; in fact it probably made it more natural.

At the end of the day, we had the photo we were looking for, and the book had a cover.

Chapter 11

It DIDN'T TAKE LONG till the strain of carrying around another baby began to take its toll on my body. As much as I loved the house we were living in at the time, it was entirely impractical for me as it had a long flight of stairs. I could cope all right if I was walking by myself because I could use the railing to pull myself up, but with a baby in my arms it was a real struggle as I tried to pull myself up with one arm and hold the baby in the other. It was difficult to say the least—not to mention dangerous!

I was used to falling over all the time, especially when I was tired and I would get 'foot drop' where I was unable to lift my foot up before taking another step. On one occasion I fell over right in the middle of the city in rush hour—I'm sure I must have looked like I had had too much to drink! I became very nervous with Charlotte in my arms as I obviously didn't want to fall down the stairs with her.

Consequently the strain on my legs and knees started to show. I was in constant pain, which I tried to ignore, but one day my right knee totally locked up so that I was unable to bend it.

Once again I rang Doctor Stephen and he convinced me that I should see another Doctor who specialised in knee injuries. I really didn't like the idea of a different doctor but I was assured by Doctor Stephen that Dr Kohan was an excellent doctor and that years ago Dr Kohan had been one of his students.

Doctor Kohan concluded that it was probable that I had a torn cartilage in my right knee and that I would need to go into hopsital for investigative surgery. It was highly probable that I had actually sustained the injury in my accident and until now it had been dormant. The added strain of carrying a baby had caused it to flare up. He also said that it was likely that my left knee would also 'go' at some stage.

I wasn't really surprised—after all, I had carried around a broken arm for six and a half years. What was a few more torn cartilages to add?

Hap had to take me into hospital for the op, while Tim looked after Annabel. It was all pretty low key and I was planning to go home that night. As usual, we had to wait some time while we were admitted, and I began to chat to the young guy who was sitting next to me, looking rather nervous.

'Are you in for an operation?' I asked.

'Yeah, on my knee,' he replied.

'Me too. What happened to you?' I enquired.

'Oh, it happened at footy. What about you?'

'Well, I'm not really sure, I think I just strained it.' It was too complicated to go into—after all, could I explain that it probably happened eight years ago in a bike accident, but I'd only just found out about it now?

We finished out checking in procedure and I was told

that I was one of the first on the list. Good news. Much to my disappointment, however, when the time came around, they had to reshuffle the list, which was a bit disappointing but obviously someone was in greater need of immediate surgery than I was. I ended up spending a lot of time sitting in my hospital room, waiting for my turn.

As I sat there, bored and restless, I started thinking about the young guy I'd been chatting to. His football career had been put on hold until his knee healed properly—if it ever did. I thought back to my sporting career, and how lucky I'd been. Apart from the minor aches and pains, I really hadn't had any serious injuries. I did have my shins operated on just prior to my accident—what a waste that had been! There was just one time, I remembered, on my bike. I closed my eyes and drifted off into another world.

I put my head down and tried not to think about the noise of the cars as they passed me, too close for comfort. I really hated riding on the road, but it was unavoidable. The roads in Sydney were not ideal for cycling, not like in Norway where I had done a bit of cycling in the past. Over there cyclists are respected, given a wide berth; indeed in most places there are special lanes to accommodate bikes.

It was different here. The safety of cyclists was not an issue to drivers. It was that odd driver that held some sort of personal vendetta against 'all' cyclists that really made riding a peril. So often when I had ridden my bike to university, I was overtaken by a car that practically pushed me to the side of the road. Even when I was riding very fast, they couldn't wait for me to move over, they just roared past with no regard for my safety.

Now I was on a very narrow stretch of road. I was pushing it to the max, I couldn't go any faster. I knew I had to keep it up till I reached a point in the road where it became wider but I was too late. From the sound behind me, I knew it wasn't a car, it was something larger, perhaps a truck. Surely he wouldn't pass here? There wasn't any room; surely he would wait the few seconds it would take to reach the wider road?

Then I felt a draft approaching and realised with dread that he was trying to pass! I kept my eyes dead ahead, not daring to look over as I knew I might overbalance. Then the side of the truck was right beside me, pushing me over, the huge wheels only inches away. Don't panic, I ordered myself, just stay on the bike.

The rear of the truck swung over; he was turning too soon. I could feel myself being pushed further over. I looked down; the road dropped away. My wheels caught the edge of the gravel then I tumbled right off the road and onto the rocky strip that lay somewhere below.

I looked up to see the truck speeding off in the distance, the driver completely unaware of what he had done. I lay there, my feet still strapped in my pedals, starting to feel an ache in my chest.

I was bruised and sore, with a cracked rib but I had escaped what could have been serious injury. My body sure did take a pounding. Not two weeks later I went in the 'Big Swim' from Palm Beach to Whale Beach. When I finished I had already decided to run back to pick up my car at my sister's house, which was thirty kilometres away! That was just a day's training for me then.

I was completely obsessed with training. It was my life. I could never have imagined myself doing anything else—I was an athlete and I loved it. Everything revolved around my sport.

When I needed to work, I would take up aerobics teaching. At one point I was teaching ten classes a week during the holidays and then at least a class a day in term, and that was in between my other training commitments. I rode my bike to the gym, and then I often stopped off at the pool on the way home. That was how I eventually got interested in triathlons, which I considered a fun way to break up the training.

I never went anywhere without my training equipment. In my car I had my roller skis, my runners, towels, a bag filled with training clothes. Everything sport-related had a purpose—even my watch was waterproof and had every function needed to record my training times.

I can still see my running tracks in my mind. I knew each one and its distance. I had driven around each course and plotted it so I was able to choose where I ran everyday. I just loved the feeling, the high, you would get after a hard training session. Nothing could beat that.

'OK, they're ready for you.'

I must have been asleep for hours! I was wheeled off and before long I was on the operation table again. When I awoke in the recovery room, my leg was quite sore and covered extensively in green hospital bandages right up to my upper thigh. I knew it must have been a relatively quick procedure as I didn't feel sick like I usually did after surgery.

It was getting quite late and I rang Hap to ask if he could come and pick me up. I certainly didn't want to spend the night in hospital if I could avoid it!

Hap had to carry me out to the car as I was unable to walk. I was told I would have to try to stay off my leg for a couple of days so I would need to use my crutches again, hopefully for the last time!

Chapter 12

As my due date rapidly approached, I was having many more problems than I had expected. I was finding the strain on my back quite unbearable; just moving around was so painful the only relief was to lie flat.

We decided to induce the baby for both the baby's sake and my own.

It was such a different scenario from Annabel's birth. Of course, knowing when you are going into labour takes away the element of surprise. On a Tuesday afternoon we dropped Annabel at Mum's place and then made our way to the hospital.

We headed upstairs to the ward where I was to have the prostaglandin gel inserted. I was relieved I was going to have the gel instead of the oxytocin drip. I had heard so many negative things about the drip and the fact it produced extreme labour contractions. The gel, I was told, stimulated a more natural birth.

By the time the paperwork was done and the gel in place, it was getting late in the afternoon. The nurse said it would probably take all night to start having an effect, so Tim might as well go home. I would ring if there was any action. As soon as I was in established labour, I could go downstairs to the birthing centre.

Not long after Tim went, I started feeling the first hints of pain. Not wanting Tim to come back in too early, I decided to get up and pace the hall, which wasn't the easiest thing to do with my mammoth bulge. It was a busy night and there were many other women doing the same thing.

If we hadn't all been pregnant, we would probably have felt silly pacing the hall in our nighties, grunting and groaning as we took occasional respite against the nearest wall. But as anyone who has given birth knows, you don't care in the slightest what anyone thinks of you while you are in labour; the only concern is getting it over with! You would give birth in the middle of Pitt St. if you had to!

Just when I believed I was really getting somewhere, the pains abated and I was left wondering what on earth was going on. Didn't this baby want to come out?

Apart from wanting to get rid of my cumbersome shape and be able to bend over once again, I was filled with anticipation as to what my new baby would be like. Would it look like Annabel—blonde, blue eyes and a complexion so fair she would need an SFP 50 plus all her life? Or would it be more like me and my side of the family, with our darker complexion and hair colouring?

I was bursting to get a look at my new baby.

I spent a frustrating night in the ward, barely able to get any sleep for, annoyingly, the pains were too strong to allow a restful night, yet not strong enough to indicate I was in full-blown labour. By morning I was disappointed and tired, but at least, I thought, I was a little closer to seeing my baby.

Wheeled downstairs in a wheelchair, I was relieved to see

the friendly and familiar faces of the birth centre and its comfortable homelike atmosphere and inviting spa. I was shown to a bedroom on the opposite side to the one I had given birth to Annabel in. The room was identical with its double bed, bassinet and comfortable chairs.

I had given Tim a call and he was on his way. I decided to wait until the pains were stronger before I jumped into the spa. By the time Tim arrived the pains were getting quite strong and I was relieved to see him. Tim is the most laid-back character I have ever met, and he never panics, so he was just the sort of person I needed around to reassure me.

I was sure now that this was it, and as the contractions became stronger I was looking forward to hearing the midwife confirm that the baby was on its way.

Then the contractions stopped.

I couldn't believe it; everything had been going along fine, then all of a sudden the contractions ceased. I was very tired by now—I had been going since the previous afternoon—and was keen to get things over with. Someone suggested the spa might make things start up again. So I got in and the contractions started but then stopped again. This was how I spent most of the day. In and out of labour. Late in the afternoon, Rosemary, the midwife, broke my waters and said that things would really speed up now. I hoped so because there was only a short amount of time before I would have to go up to the labour ward to have the oxytocin drip inserted—once the waters are broken, it is vital to get the baby out as soon as possible.

Some time later there was still no change. I was exhausted, frustrated and worried that the baby might be getting distressed.

'Sorry Janine, looks like we'll have to take you up to the labour ward,' Rosemary decided eventually.

I had been half expecting it, but it was still hard to take. I did what any exhausted pregnant woman would do at this stage, I started to cry. I was so disappointed. I wanted to have my baby in the cosy birth centre, just as I had with Annabel, and now I was relegated to that sterile, impersonal ward upstairs.

With Tim reassuring me, I was put in a wheelchair and wheeled into the lift. The labour ward was just what I had expected. Instead of having the birthing equipment cleverly concealed by homely pieces of furniture, the utensils were in plain view.

The staff were helpful, however. Rosemary had escorted me upstairs to bridge the gap between the birth centre and the labour ward, and she left only when she felt I was settled down. The nurse looking after me inserted the drip line and switched on the oxytocin. It felt terribly restrictive being tied to the stand. Up until now I had been having mild contractions, more annoying than painful because they wouldn't get any stronger. They were like severe period cramps—hardly what I knew labour pains to amount to.

Some time early in the evening, much to my surprise, my sister Kim came bounding in with two beers in her hand.

'What are you doing here?' I asked.

'Well, when I heard you were still in labour, I thought I might be able to give you a hand. I thought Tim might need a break.'

What about me? I thought grumpily, but it was good to see another familiar face.

Thinking Tim might appreciate a cold drink, Kim had brought him in a beer. Looking back, it was the most ridiculous scene. Me, the whale, sitting at the bedside, with my drip in, panting every time I had one of my mini contractions, while Tim and Kim sat enjoying their beers and discussing the day. When the contraction had passed I would interrupt and fill Kim in on any details Tim had left out.

Then Tim discovered the gas next to my bed and, his curiosity getting the best of him, picked up the mask and pretended to suck on it. I was just taking a photo of him when the nurse walked in. 'Hey, I think it's Janine who's supposed to be having that,' she laughed.

I thought it was going to be another long night, so when Kim offered to stay I said she might as well go home and get some sleep. She left and the nurse came by to check how I was. Still nothing dramatic happening.

It turned out I had picked one of the busiest nights on record. The labour ward was filled to the brim. The doctors on duty were flat out trying to attend to all the patients, and all I could hear were screams as the women gave birth. It was a sound I had become quite used to in the hours since I had arrived.

'I'm going to break your waters,' the nurse said and began giving me an internal examination.

I told her they had already done that downstairs.

'Well it doesn't look like it. Sometimes they can nick some of the membrane but not enough.'

I was desperate to get the birth over. I had been at the hospital over twenty-four hours and hadn't slept more than a few hours in that time. I had had it.

She pierced the membrane and then in a worried voice exclaimed, 'Uh oh, it looks like meconium.'

That was the wrong thing to say to an exhausted woman in labour. 'What do you mean?' I asked in a panic, knowing meconium indicated the baby was in distress and it was important to get it out immediately.

Before my panic could develop into hysteria, another nurse came in to look and said it wasn't meconium at all, and there was no need to worry. However, I had been in labour a long time and what they really had to do now was turn the drip up to get things going quicker.

With my waters officially broken and the oxytocin increased, the contractions came on with such a rush that I was taken totally by surprise. There was no gentle lead-up like a normal contraction, it just hit me like a sledgehammer and stayed that way for over a minute. It was the most excruciating pain, not only for its intensity but because there was no peak which meant there was no lull. Once it started I knew it would stay that way for a long time, and when it finally finished I would wait in dreaded silence for the next attack. The pain I had experienced with Annabel seemed mild in comparison.

'What's the time?' I asked Tim in between contractions.

'Five minutes since the last time you asked.'

I couldn't believe it; it seemed as though I had been doing this for an eternity. In fact, it had only been twenty minutes since the drip had been turned up.

In less than thirty seconds another contraction came. I grabbed the bed, put my head down and began to yell into the mattress. The pain in my back was unbearable. I remembered what it was like with Annabel now and asked myself why on earth I was doing it all over again.

My back felt as though it was breaking in half. I reached for the buzzer. 'Get the doctor. I need something. *Help!*' I screamed.

Tim grabbed me to stop me from falling.

'Janine, calm down, you're all right,' he said calmly.

'No, I need an epidural, get me an epidural!' I shouted aggressively.

'You can't have an epidural, you know that.'

I didn't really need to be told that, but I was desperate. I would have taken anything!

'Call the nurse, get someone, the pain's too much! Get some

painkillers.' I was hysterical by now and starting to panic. My entire body was being torn open and nobody cared.

'Honey, you're about to have the baby,' Tim said.

'*Help*, someone, *please!*' I screamed at the top of my voice.

Nobody appeared. I felt utterly abandoned.

The back pain was extreme. Tim had to dig his knee into my back to try to distract me.

'Harder!' I yelled, thinking I couldn't take this anymore. 'Help, someone help!' I screamed even louder. I was getting furious now.

It seemed everyone was giving birth at the same time. Tim was running out to get help, when the nurse appeared. She looked surprised at the state I was in. She had figured it would be a while before I was ready to deliver.

Tim helped me down to a stool and she examined me.

'Oh, wow, you're fully dilated, we'll have to call someone quickly ... I'll call Sue back!' she said urgently.

Sue, my obstetrician, had only just delivered a baby and was on her way home. She would have to turn around and make her way back to the hospital.

Poor Tim was having to hold the full weight of my body as I leaned on him for support, and at the same time was pressing his knee into my back, which felt as though it was breaking in two.

By the time Sue made it to the ward, there was action everywhere. I acknowledged her but was finding it hard to be polite. 'Please can't you take the drip out now?' I pleaded. The drip was causing the intense contractions which were draining all my strength, or what was left of it after such an inordinate time in labour.

'I'm sorry, Janine, but we need it to stay in until after the baby is born, just in case of complications,' Sue explained.

They put a mirror between my legs so I could see but I really didn't care, I just wanted it to be over.

'One more, Janine, it's almost there,' I heard someone say. All I wanted was for Tim to push harder into my back. I couldn't think, I was so exhausted.

Sue worked methodically until she had the baby's head in her grasp, and before I knew it the body slid effortlessly out into her hands. The relief was instantaneous.

I was slumped against Tim's body when someone placed a little ball of baby, wrapped in green hospital cloth, in my arms. I had no energy to move or even hold the baby properly.

I looked down at my new daughter. She was fair like Annabel and just as beautiful. Strangely, she looked as though she was smiling. She actually looked directly in my eyes.

I knew this was the beginning of another love affair.

'Have you got a name for her?' Sue asked.

'Yes,' I said. 'Charlotte Rose.' And then I handed her to Tim for I had no strength to hold her any longer.

I felt content, and now it was time to rest.

As Tim turned I could see his shirt was covered in sweat, but he didn't care, he was absorbed in his new baby daughter.

Chapter 13

I was sitting in the birth centre holding Charlotte when Annabel and Tim bounded in through the door.

The look on Annabel's face is something I will treasure for a long time. She ran over to me and looked down at the baby with a mixture of fascination and wonder. She didn't say a word, just gently stroked the fine layer of down on Charlotte's head.

I asked her if she would like to hold her sister and she said she would. She sat down, dwarfed by the large chair, and I gently placed the tiny bundle in her arms. It was the first time Annabel had touched or indeed seen such a young baby, and she was in awe.

I was bursting with pride and love for these two little people of mine. It was something so special to see Annabel with her new sister. The family had grown and I couldn't wait to get home with Charlotte to begin her new life with us.

I had no idea how much more work an extra baby was!

One more person and the amount of washing quadrupled. Every time I sat down to feed Charlotte, Annabel needed something that couldn't wait one more second. Not naturally very organised, I was quickly forced to become so just to get through each day.

Thank goodness Tim was not flying bank runs and could spend more time at home this time around. He and I shared caring for Charlotte as much as possible so we could both spend plenty of time with Annabel. We were well aware of the dangers of a new baby getting all the attention and wanted to avoid any animosity Annabel might develop towards her new sister. I was relieved to see she was overjoyed with the new addition to the family and wanted to help out as much as possible. That was wonderful of course, although I was a bit nervous about her trying to lift and carry her when we were out of the room.

Before long she became adept at caring for her sister and the household ran fairly smoothly. That's not to say it wasn't always a mess—it was—but at least we were always fed . . . and sometimes clean!

Just as I was adding a few final touches to the book before it was printed, I had a phone call from Jane. She had been offered a job with another major publisher, and, as it was a promotion, she had reluctantly decided to take it.

It took me by surprise. I completely understood Jane's decision—she would have been crazy to have passed up such an opportunity—but she had been my sounding post throughout the writing of my book and now I felt very alone. It was Jane who had first heard my story, and she who had seized the opportunity to sign me up, believing with great vigour that the book would be a success.

I hadn't had any contact with anyone else during the

writing of my book and wondered whether, without Jane there, my book would still get the support it needed. I didn't express these doubts to Jane, instead I just wished her all the best and said I would miss her.

Around this time, I had a phone call from a friend who was involved with an organisation called the Queen's Trust which every year held a forum for one hundred young Australians, aged in their early twenties, who were considered the leaders of the future.

Selection to attend the forum was extremely competitive and only the most promising of those who applied were chosen. They would come from all over Australia to attend a week of lectures from eminent Australians in the business world, the arts, health and politics. The conference was closed every year by someone who had an inspiring story to share, someone who had faced innumerable challenges and who could offer these young Australians some valuable insights.

For the past few years they had had Tim Macartney-Snape talk to the group along with another speaker from a different field. I of course knew Tim as the first Australian to ascend Mount Everest and I held him in great esteem. So I was more than a little humbled when I was asked to be the other speaker at the forum. Tim had achieved something of such great courage and magnitude, I was honoured even to be considered to share the platform with him.

The forum, to be held in Brisbane in September, was going to be something altogether different from Toastmasters. Even though there was no fee involved, I considered this to be a professional job and wanted to give the best presentation I could, especially as I would be speaking with Tim, who did this for a living.

I needed to prepare a speech approximately thirty to

forty minutes long, so first I typed it out and then stuck the pages together in one continual piece so that I could see what I was trying to say. The house was one long sheet of my life story!

It wasn't just a matter of telling my story, I had to leave the audience with a valuable message. The problem was, which one? I felt by now I had quite a few!

Since it was my flying that had got me back on my feet, I decided to leave them with an aeronautical formula I believed would give them something to think about.

At the Sydney Aerobatic School the pilots don't wear the standard uniform of blue pants, a white pilot's shirt and a tie. But nobody told me that, so on the day I started working there I bounded into the building wearing the regulation garb. When the other pilots saw me they all exclaimed, 'What on earth are you wearing?'

I looked down and rather shyly said, 'My uniform', wondering what I had done wrong.

I hadn't been informed that the uniform at SAS was in fact *no* uniform! The school's philosophy was that comfort was essential and that a uniform actually made flying very uncomfortable. The pilots needed to wear big boots so that they could kick in with the rudder when needed. And a tie might end up in the pilot's face and make seeing difficult. When the instructor can't see, you definitely have a problem! This wasn't for show, this was 'real' flying and it was inappropriate to dress formally to teach someone how to roll or flick an aircraft upside down.

Our 'uniform' was a pair of jeans, the older the better, a T-shirt and a pair of solid boots. The T-shirt was of our own choice until Tim came up with the bright idea of designing a school shirt. We had some T-shirts printed with the words *How's your attitude?* on one side of the chest with the SAS logo—an upside-down aeroplane—underneath.

It became an instant conversation piece.

Whenever anyone saw the T-shirt, they would comment. Of course, to those familiar with aviation lingo, it made perfect sense because attitude is the relationship of the nose of the aircraft to the horizon. However, for the layman, it means something quite different.

As I thought about my speech I remembered a formula that is used every day in flying and one that is familiar to every pilot.

Attitude + Power = Performance.

Attitude, in simple terms, is the picture you see out of the front of the aircraft when you are flying. Power is the thrust that comes from the engine, and performance is what you want to get out of the aircraft.

For example, with the aircraft I was teaching in, if I wanted to fly straight and level, then I would set a straight and level attitude out the front, which would give me a view of two-thirds sky and one-third terrain. I would set the power of the engine to 2500 rpm and would get a performance of 115 knots.

This is a mathematical formula, so it works every time, and that is the beauty of it. There's no guesswork; just follow the formula and you'll get the results, simple as that.

There is so much in this formula that is analogous to life. My attitude expressed in my choice of title for my book—*Never Tell Me Never*—had taken me beyond all expectations, my own and everyone else's. I had been to the edge and back again because I refused to listen to what others expected from me. I have always believed that there is something worth fighting for and it was precisely this attitude that got me through the toughest fight of my life.

Of course, there are so many other qualities that might make up a positive attitude. For example, the ability to see the good in everything, or the determination that keeps us hanging in there even when the odds are stacked against us, or the tendency to remain optimistic even when faced with apparently insurmountable obstacles.

However, a good attitude alone won't guarantee success. It requires a great deal of hard work to make something of nothing. Although I had tremendous support during my rehabilitation, when it came down to it, it was up to me to make something out of my situation. Nobody else was going to get me back on my feet, nobody could do the work for me. The power had to come from me alone. Just as the engine in the aeroplane provides the energy to get the aircraft in the air, so we need to put that power behind everything we do. I call it the three Ds. First we must have the desire, then the determination and the dedication to work hard to succeed at whatever we do.

The level of performance is the direct result of our attitude and the power we exert. A bad attitude and no effort will inevitably result in a bad performance. But with the right attitude and plenty of hard work, there is no limit to our performance.

As I was writing these words I realised how important it is to have something to strive for. It is no use using the formula without clear goals in mind. It was my desire to learn to fly that had got me out of bed each day and given me something to aim for.

In aviation we talk about way points, which are compass points or landmarks we pass as we travel from place to place. In our lives we need way points. We need things to strive for, whether they are personal goals, business or sporting goals. Without them we fly around with no direction or flight plan and cannot live up to our potential.

We must first decide upon a goal and then apply the formula; Attitude + Power = Performance.

These were the things I wanted to talk about. Flying was my life and it had taught me so much. This was what I would share with my audience.

As the day approached, I came down with a dreadful cold. My throat was sore, I had a niggling cough and I felt extremely tired. I just wanted to curl up in bed and go to sleep. I couldn't of course. The talk had been months in preparation and I could hardly pull out at such short notice. I would just have to stock up on cough tablets and cope as best I could.

The day before the speech, leaving Annabel with Mum, Tim, baby Charlotte and I piled into the aircraft and flew to Brisbane. There we made our way to the hotel where I went over my notes for the conference the following day.

I had been so looking forward to spending the night away at a big hotel with Tim; it was almost going to be like a second honeymoon. We hadn't had a night alone since Annabel had been born. So much for plans!

I spent the entire night trying to get some sleep but my throat was getting sorer by the minute. I sucked a few lozenges but to no avail. By the morning my throat was so inflamed I could barely utter a few words. Just what I needed—laryngitis! I was forced to speak in a whisper for fear of losing my voice altogether.

Outside the venue I noticed Tim Macartney-Snape getting out of the car next to us. I managed to say hello, explaining that I had a bit of a cold and from there Tim had to take over the talking. We were introduced to the organising committee and then I was led through a maze of corridors into the auditorium where a talk was in progress. It looked very full and everyone was obviously engrossed.

Tim Macartney-Snape was on before me so I sat at the back of the auditorium and listened with great interest as he recalled some of his magnificent accomplishments. All too soon it was my turn. My throat was raspy by now but at least the cough wasn't too bad. I was introduced and made my way to the podium.

I tried to raise my voice but my throat was so aggravated that I began to cough. I felt very self-conscious. I continued to talk and the more I talked, the more I coughed. It was one of those niggling, tickly coughs that the more you try not to cough, the more you cough.

I struggled to get a few words out, then I leant over to take a sip of water thinking it would help, but I soon discovered that cold water on a sore throat just aggravates it even more!

I looked out over the one hundred faces resting on every word I was trying to say. The only thing I could do was make a joke about the whole situation and get through my speech the best I could.

I noticed a man stand up at the back of the room. Uh oh, someone was leaving already! As he began to make his way to the front of the auditorium, I realised he was coming up on stage.

'I thought these might help,' he said as he handed me some lozenges. Everyone laughed, me included. 'They're extra strong.'

As I took the packet and popped one in my mouth, I told the audience I had been through some big challenges in my life but nothing compared to this!

I made it through the speech, coughing and spluttering all the way. The lozenges didn't help much but the gesture was nice. The audience gave me a good reception and afterwards I stayed for morning tea and talked with many of the young people at the forum. They were all eager to read my book and it felt strange to be talking about something that I hadn't seen yet. I still couldn't believe I had written a book and certainly didn't feel like an author.

Chapter 14

ONCE THE BOOK was on the shelves, I would be required to go on a tour of Australia to promote it. This would involve literary luncheons, radio interviews and television appearances. I soon discovered that it isn't enough merely to write a book, you have to be able to sell it too!

One of the highest rating shows on television is '60 Minutes' but I was told it would be virtually impossible to get my story on the show because they are very selective. I dismissed the idea until I received a phone call from my friend Adrian. He was always interested to know how the book was going and in the course of the discussion I happened to mention the pending publicity tour.

'Hey, I know one of the producers from '60 Minutes', why don't I give him a ring and see if he's interested?' he offered.

'Wow, that would be fantastic, Ado,' I exclaimed. It was a long shot, but it was worth a try.

Not long after that one of the producers at '60 Minutes', Stephen Taylor, called and asked if he could meet me. I was surprised—I hadn't expected a response so quickly.

We talked briefly and made a date. I guessed it was going to be a vetting procedure to gauge whether or not I was a suitable subject for a story.

When Stephen came over I was pleasantly surprised. I had expected him to be older than me, but in fact I was older than him. He looked far too young to be a television producer. He was very pleasant and I felt at ease immediately. He asked me about the accident and we talked for some time. He said that regardless of how he felt about the story's suitability, it would have to go back to the executive producer, who would then decide if they could run with it. Before he could make a decision however, he said he would like to read part of what I had written.

I had received the completed draft of my book a few months before, but apart from Jane and myself, nobody had read it. Not even Tim. He had been given the job of reading my original chapters after I wrote each day, so I hadn't asked him to read it again. I was a bit sick of reading it over and over myself! I knew Mum was keen to read the manuscript, but I wanted her to read it when it was a finished book, cover and all.

If I gave it to Stephen, he would be the first person to read the book objectively. I was a bit reluctant but I finally agreed, thinking it would take him the best part of a week to finish it and so didn't expect to hear from him too soon.

To my surprise I received a phone call from Stephen early the next morning. He told me he had started reading last night and hadn't been able to stop; in fact, he had finished the book in one session.

I breathed a sigh of relief: I had passed the test!

He was keen to put it up to the executive producer and would be in contact as soon as he got the go-ahead. I didn't have long to wait. The story was approved and Stephen arranged for Charles Wooley to cover it. I was pleased but my publishers were ecstatic!

Arrangements were underway to get some action shots of me on the snow, and the prospect of hitting the slopes again reminded me of my first attempt at skiing after the accident. It was just my luck that a junior racing clinic happened to be on in Falls Creek that week, so I had to go through the humiliating process of trying to ski in front of them. I had convinced myself that I would at least be able to ski at a recreational level but, to my absolute horror, I couldn't even stand. With no feeling in my legs, and no lower-leg muscles, my balance was atrocious. Once again I had underestimated the extent of my injuries.

After getting over the initial shock of just how difficult it was going to be, I set about torturing my body to the point of being bruised black and blue.

After that I spent several seasons driving down to stay at Cooma Hut where I was a member. All of my friends were there which stirred up a mixture of emotions. As much as I enjoyed seeing them, it hurt terribly to see them ski off in the morning for a training session and know that I couldn't go with them. Although I never let on to them, I was aching inside for what I had lost.

On one particular day I was absolutely determined I was going to make it around a ten kilometre track to the Nordic shelter even if it killed me. The only skis I had were my racing skis, which didn't make it any easier as they were so narrow and with my balance I had little chance of staying on. Despite this, I had to give it a go.

I negotiated the first part of the track, which is quite flat, without too many problems. I probably looked as though I had never been on skis before, but I didn't care. I got up the first hill, then came my first real challenge—a downhill. It was a straight run down with two sets of tracks.

Normally I would have got into a tuck without a second thought but now it was a different matter.

I reasoned that all I had to do was keep my skis in the tracks, which were quite deep, and I would be fine. I launched myself with reckless abandon. I could feel the speed increasing, and knew I was completely out of control. There was nothing I could do. My feet started to wobble.

Bang!

I rolled and rolled. I felt something hit my face. I couldn't stop and ended up face down in the snow, hardly the most dignified pose.

I had to lie still for a minute or two to get my bearings. It had been quite a fall. I looked around to see what was left of my skis and saw that one stock had been snapped in half. They were carbon fibre poles and very strong—I had never broken one before.

My face was aching. I put my hand up and saw it was bleeding.

I could see some other skiers looking down at me, wondering if I was OK. I gave them a little wave and got myself on my feet. I felt terrible.

Pulling myself together, I picked up my broken stock and continued on my way.

I was going to finish the ten kilometres no matter what!

I plodded and felt my way around until I reached the final hill. The S bends. Even before my accident these were a challenge; the only way was straight down and you just had to go for it. There was nowhere to slow down for the corners or the trees and the course rolled out to a long hill at the end.

I stopped at the top, my stomach churning. How on earth was I ever going to get down there? As nervous as I was, I knew if I didn't finish I would regret it forever. It couldn't be any worse than the fall I had already had, I reasoned.

Approaching the trees in a snowplough to keep my speed down, I knew I would now just have to let myself go. I put my skies parallel and got into a modified tuck. So far so good.

With my legs shaking violently, I made it around the corner. I was out of control but that didn't matter because at least I hadn't hit any trees. Down the straight, I knew sooner or later I was going to crash but for now I was in a clearing.

Bang!

Down I went again. At least I didn't break a pole this time. I dusted myself off, and made my way down the trail again. I knew I was almost home; it was mostly flat from here on.

I rounded the last bend. I could see the Nordic shelter. I put my head down and double-poled to the finish. I had made it.

There was no-one there, I was all alone.

I took off my skis and carried my broken pole inside. I was absolutely exhausted. But I was over the moon—I had skied the ten kilometre track.

When I glanced in the mirror, I realised I looked like I had been in a fight. My right eye was bruised and swollen and there was blood all over my face!

I have pushed myself to the limit to get back on skis again. As I have no calf muscles, I have to support myself with my upper legs. This places incredible pressure on my thighs and knees and after a short time they begin burning up with the strain of having to do all the work. My poor body has suffered a lot as a result. However, I now get a great deal of satisfaction at being able to ski socially with Tim who is a keen cross-country skier. Tim loves to tour, to go out on the range, so I have packed my racing skis away for a more sensible pair of touring skis which are wider and much more forgiving.

Downhill skiing is much easier for me though, as the boots give me more support than cross-country boots. We have started the girls skiing and Annabel is a natural. She is a real daredevil and has no fear whatsoever. I have to stop all the time to give my legs a rest, whilst Annabel, on the other hand, never wants to stop. 'Hurry up, Mummy,' she yells, whenever I fall behind. Charlotte had skis on when she was one. This year she was skiing the rope tow all by herself and feeling very grown up, all two and a half years of her!

Annabel and Charlotte love the snow so much. I know that all the hard work and pushing myself hasn't been in vain. It has enabled me to ski at a level where I can enjoy myself with my girls.

At that time my problem wasn't getting onto skis for the '60 Minutes' cameras, it was how I was going to get away for a couple of days—I was still breastfeeding, you see. Taking Charlotte with me was a logistical nightmare so I decided I would just have to take a breast pump and express.

I was booked to go down to Perisher during race week, which was ideal because I knew some of my friends would be down there then and would be only too happy to put on an exhibition for the cameras. Stephen told me we would be first going out to Prince Henry Hospital, where I had been a patient, to film some hospital footage. After that we would be going out to the airport to catch a charter aircraft down to Cooma Airport.

Without hesitation I told him that I would gladly catch a regular public transport flight down to Cooma but I wouldn't do so in a charter aircraft.

'But you're a pilot!' he exclaimed in disbelief.

'That's exactly why I won't go. Not unless I'm flying myself and I know the aircraft and who has been maintaining it,' I explained. I had seen too many accidents not to know what went on in the charter business. Stephen had to arrange for me to fly down with Eastern Australia Airlines, the company that Tim was flying for, before I was happy.

I packed my bag and said a tearful goodbye to Tim, Annabel and Charlotte. I knew I would soon have to travel without them for the book launch, but I still hated being apart from them, even for two days.

Being back at the hospital was like going back through a time warp. Although it had been years since I had been there, everything was so familiar it felt like yesterday. Approaching the front gates, I noticed the Chinese restaurant across the road where Dad used to buy my dinner some nights when the hospital food was too unbearable to eat.

Mum and Dad must have come through these gates so often to visit me, now it was my turn. I thought about all the patients who would be lying there in the spinal unit, wondering what sort of day it was outside, not able to move or even glance out of the window to see. I looked up; it was a beautiful, sunny day.

A few people were leaving the unit as I walked in. They looked solemn and I felt a sadness for them. I had come such a long way but I still remembered.

Most of the nursing staff were unfamiliar to me. I wasn't surprised; the turnover rate in spinal wards is quite rapid as it takes a heavy toll on staff. I managed to find a few people I remembered and told them what I was doing there. I felt uneasy returning to film inside the ward in case it upset anyone, and I was hoping it would all be over as soon as possible.

By now Stephen had arrived and he introduced me to Nick, the cameraman, and Micky, the sound engineer.

Micky chatted incessantly and told jokes, and I got the feeling that we were all going to have a lot of fun together.

Charles Wooley finally arrived, and we were introduced very briefly before being whisked inside to do a shoot. We didn't have much time as the crew had to travel to North Shore Hospital to do an interview with Doctor Yeo after we had finished here. Then they had to get back to the airport to catch the charter flight to Cooma before dark.

We got some shots inside the ward then went into the acute ward where I was surprised to find my old bed vacant. I sat down on it and Charles asked me some questions about my hospital stay while Nick filmed us. It was rather bizarre being back in such different circumstances.

We were told there was a patient who needed cheering up and I was asked if I would mind talking to him. The hope was that if he saw me, knowing I had once been a patient, it might give him some encouragement, particularly since his injuries weren't as bad as mine had been.

I was happy to oblige, of course, and spent some time chatting to him about his accident. I think it helped him, if only because it relieved the boredom of lying in a hospital bed day after day.

Next we went to another unit where we could shoot some scenes of me lying in bed without disturbing any other patients. Stephen had me put on one of the hospital gowns and lie in bed while one of the nurses attached every sort of contraption possible to my body. I had tubes in my mouth and nose, which wasn't exactly comfortable! I had mock drips on my arm, and Stephen even wanted to put the oxygen mask over my face but I protested.

Nick shot some footage as I lay there trying to be still and not laugh. Meanwhile, Micky was busy getting the sound right. In his hand was a huge contraption that

Speaking at an official Westpac Lifesaver Helicopter function.
Below: Me with Bob Joss, Head of Westpac Bank.

Tim manning the front desk at the Sydney Aerobatic School.

Tim and his hot dog stand – the best hot dogs in the world.

Surprising Elizabeth in Mudgee while doing a charter flight.

With Elizabeth, my soul mate.

Re-enacting my accident for the '60 Minutes' story.
Below and opposite: Australia's leading stunt man takes
Debbie through the 'accident'.

The re-enactment was chillingly realistic. Debbie ended up bruised and battered by the end of the day.

Steven Taylor *(front)* and Mickey Breen checking out the scene for '60 Minutes'.

My bike after being tossed off the car hundreds of times.

Me in full flight at a speaking engagement.

Speaking and signing
books at the ACCA
function.

Above: signing books at the ACCA function.

Left: Signing books after the Amway conference in Melbourne.
The queue went halfway around the Melbourne Tennis Centre.

Tim and I kayaking on Sydney Harbour.

In a Robin
aerobatic
aircraft.

Flying in
formation.

Cailin Piper, a future
Qantas pilot.

Me with Rebecca Saxton at the Australian
Defence Force Academy.

Suzi Duncan, Anthony Bonaccurso and Ian Brown.
Anthony had just completed his first solo.

An extremely friendly monkey in Ubud, Bali.

Feeding the bats in Ubud, Bali. These bats love Fanta!

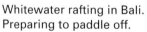

Whitewater rafting in Bali. Preparing to paddle off.

Patrick Hamilton and his class singing *Janine's Song.*

Annabel shyly answering questions for the class.

Mr Hamilton's Class of '96, St Benedict's Primary School, Edgeworth.

looked very threatening but in fact it was only the mike. He was continually joking around and had a mean sense of humour. He was always making me laugh, which was a problem when I was supposed to be sick in bed!

Charles had already left but before he did he happened to mention, in passing, the charter flight we were catching.

'Oh, I'm not going on that,' I told him.

'What do you mean?' he asked.

'I'm going down with Easterns.'

'What? You're a pilot aren't you, what's wrong with the aircraft I'm going on?' Charles shrieked. He was already nervous enough about flying and now to learn that I wasn't trusting enough to fly down in a small charter flight ... 'Taylor, I'm going to kill you!' were his last words as he left in a taxi to interview Doctor Yeo.

I landed in Cooma with not much daylight left. It had been hours since I had breastfed and by now I was feeling extremely full. I knew that before I could catch the taxi to Perisher I would have to go to the ladies and express or I would explode! I collected my bag and went to meet the driver who was to pick me up. I gave him my bag and politely asked if he would mind waiting while I went to the ladies to express some milk.

He looked at me blankly and then suddenly became extremely embarrassed. 'Oh sure, go ahead, whatever you need, I'll wait here.'

I raced into the bathroom and got out my pump. I was so full—now I know what Dolly Parton feels like! I was very very sore. It took me a good ten minutes before I could leave in comfort and make my way out to the taxi.

I wasn't sure whether the driver had understood what I was doing but he didn't say much. I guess it was the first time one of his passengers had had to express some milk before travelling!

Arriving at the lodge as darkness fell, I unpacked, had a bath and a cup of tea, and then had to use my pump again. After dinner with the boys and a drink with my good friends Tim and Fiona, I went back to the lodge for an early night. I knew if I didn't get some sleep I would be a wreck in the morning. And besides, this was my only opportunity to get a good night's rest without waking for a baby, and I was going to take full advantage of it.

I was mistaken. By taking the breast pump along I had created a monster. The more I expressed, the more milk I started to produce and the more often I had to express, and so the vicious cycle went on. I got hardly any sleep that night as I was so uncomfortable I had to keep getting up and going to the bathroom.

The next morning it was blowing a gale. Charles wasn't impressed. 'Great, I've never been on skis before and there's a blizzard outside!' he complained. But he had a smile on his face and I suspected that he secretly couldn't wait to have a go.

The previous night I had arranged for friends to meet us at the Nordic shelter where most of the filming would be done. Once there I helped Charles put on his skis. It was an absolute scream, I don't think I have seen anything so funny in quite a while. I was bad enough trying to balance on skis, but next to Charles I was a real pro. Charles was attempting to talk and ski at the same time, which was difficult enough, but the wind factor was so extreme we were almost skiing backwards.

Whilst Nick filmed an interview with some of the skiers, I took the opportunity to get some practice in. I was determined not to fall over too often in front of my friends and was happy as long as I could manage to stay on my feet and make some progress, but it took the utmost concentration, particularly since I couldn't feel what my feet were doing.

Charles and I watched as Stephen got some footage of my friends skiing through the trees. It was still difficult to stand by and just not be able to join in. However, the pain that would have once been so strong, was now bearable. I felt an overwhelming contentment with my life. Time had passed and healed so many of the wounds, and my new role as wife, mother and writer had given me a great sense of purpose and belonging. The paradox was that as much as I wanted to ski, I also wanted to stay exactly where I was.

By lunchtime Stephen was satisfied that he had all the shots he wanted. Nick and Micky were then given a few hours off, and since they had brought their downhill skis with them, they wasted no time in hitting the slopes with Stephen. Charles and I opted for a more sedate lunch in a restaurant overlooking the wind-blown slopes.

We met up at the lodge late in the afternoon as we all had to make tracks back to the airport. Charles had been forthright in telling Stephen that he was definitely not catching the charter flight back to Sydney, and had booked himself a seat on the flight with me. He was good company and we hadn't stopped talking since lunch so I didn't mind at all.

It was getting dark now and the weather wasn't looking good.

'It's pretty windy, isn't it?' Charles said apprehensively.

'Don't worry, Charles, we're flying with Easterns, we'll be fine.'

He was somewhat reassured by looking at the ticket with the Qantas logo emblazoned on the front; after all, they were the safest airline in the world! Just ask Dustin Hoffman!

At the airport we bumped into James Packer who had just flown in on his own Lear jet for a skiing holiday with some friends. I recognised one of them as Jennifer Flavin. He came over and introduced himself to Charles and asked what he was doing in Cooma. Charles told him they had been doing a story on a young lady who had been in a horrific accident, and then introduced me. We made some small talk before he was whisked off by his friends for the snowfields and Charles and I were called for our flight.

Walking out onto the tarmac, I straightaway realised something wasn't right. The aircraft we were boarding wasn't an Easterns' Jetstream or Dash-8. It was a Metro, a prop aircraft of slightly smaller proportions. As I got closer I noticed how shabby the pilot was. He had no epaulettes on his shirt, which wouldn't seem too out of place on a bank run, but for a regular public transport flight was highly unprofessional.

'What airline are you with?' I enquired when I reached the aircraft.

'Oh, it's a small airline based in_____,' he said.

My heart sunk. It was the same company Tim had worked for and resigned from some years ago because of their dangerous procedures and overworking of the pilots.

I looked at Charles in disbelief.

'Don't tell me Tim worked for this company too?' he said mockingly.

'Well, actually he did, and they wouldn't exactly be my first choice of airline.'

Charles glared at me. There was only one thing to do and that was to laugh, the irony was too much. This was the only flight to Sydney and we had to get back. All I could think was that we would probably have been safer catching the charter flight back with the others.

As we boarded, I could see the worry in the other

passengers' faces. They believed that they had bought a ticket with Qantas and this was a very small aircraft. Fortunately for them, ignorance is bliss and they had no idea what sort of company owned the aircraft. I knew that, only recently, one of their aircraft had crashed. I was tempted to get off and wait till the morning.

I had seen so many bad things happening in the industry that I knew it was only a matter of time before there was a full-scale investigation. I probably had more flying experience than the pilot, I realised, and wondered if he knew what a shonky airline he was working for.

With a groan and protest from the engine we were finally airborne; everything seemed to rattle and I prayed the maintenance was up to scratch. I looked over at Charles and he was glaring at me.

'If we ever touch down in Sydney, I am going to kick your backside,' he said.

'If we ever get there, I will gladly accept,' I laughed. He laughed too—there wasn't much else to do.

We did make it to Sydney safely; mind you, there wasn't much talking going on in the aircraft. When we alighted, I told Charles he was welcome to give me that kick, and he did!

As much as we joked about the incident, it was something that should never have happened. A charter company should never have been called to fill in for a major airline, particularly not a charter company with such a bad reputation. When I got home and told Tim what had happened, he was absolutely furious, and the next day he went into the office to inform his boss.

As a result, that was the last time that particular company was used in such a capacity again and Charles vowed to do a story on the procedures of the charter industry.

Stephen was keen to get some coverage of me flying, unlike poor Charles, who would have to fly with me. He was absolutely petrified of flying in small aircraft and the last thing he wanted to do was, to quote him, 'go flying with a girl who had no feeling in her legs'!

I met the crew at the airport on the arranged day. Stephen had already looked over the aircraft and met Noel from SAS to discuss what would be required. He arranged to hire a helicopter for the shoot so that he could get aerial footage of me flying in the Robin.

The Robin already had a video-camera system installed inside the cockpit as Noel used the aircraft for what he called ACES, or air combat experience school. This was where someone who had no flying experience at all could hire an aircraft with an instructor and actually go dogfighting! And of course they would get the video as a memory of their flight.

When I saw Charles I noticed he was looking a bit pale.

'I hope you know what you're doing, Shepherd. I'm not looking forward to this.'

'Oh don't worry, Charles, it'll be great fun. I haven't been flying for ages, and I'm really looking forward to this.'

I don't think that comment instilled a lot of confidence in him.

I did my pre-flight with Charles looking on and making a few tongue-in-cheek comments. We climbed into the aircraft and he continued to talk while Nick filmed.

'So how do you manage to feel where the pedals are when you don't have any feeling in your legs?' he asked slightly anxiously.

I looked at him and smiled. 'Actually, I just put my feet on the pedals and the rest is pot luck.'

He looked more nervous. I laughed.

I taxied to the runway, got my clearance and gently

raised the nose of the aircraft. Before long we were over the training area at Bankstown and Charles was looking worse for wear.

I told him I was going to do a few pre-aerobatic checks and then we would be ready to do some manoeuvres. He looked worried and I concluded that this was just his manner for the cameras. I was sure he was secretly enjoying it. I had got to know Charles well enough by now to know he liked to play it up somewhat.

I thought I would start with a simple, gentle manoeuvre, a loop.

'OK, you ready? Here we go.' I pulled back smoothly on the stick and watched as the horizon disappeared from view. All we could see was sky. I put in a touch of right rudder over the top to keep the loop straight and as I saw the ground approaching beneath us, I held onto the pressure until we finished the loop and I felt the bump that comes from hitting your own slipstream.

I looked at Charles; the expression on his face was beyond description. He was such an actor, I thought. The camera would be capturing every expression and he was really playing up to it.

Now I was going to do a stall turn. I cleared the area and pulled the aircraft up to a perfect vertical climb. Watching the airspeed, I kept the left wing straight with the rudder, and then when the airspeed dropped to forty knots, I booted in enough left rudder to turn the nose around its axis and followed through with aileron and forward stick.

We turned and headed straight down for the ground, a perfect vertical line down. The speed built up and I kept the stick pressure on to keep a straight line. Eighty knots, pull out and reduce power.

'Wow, that was great fun!' I yelled.

'Oh, I feel sick,' Charles said. 'That's enough, can we go back now?'

I was sure he was only kidding. 'Oh come on, Charles, we haven't got enough for the cameras yet. Stephen said to do quite a few manoeuvres.'

After a few more manoeuvres Charles became insistent that we return to the aerodrome. 'Please, I'll do anything, just get me down. I'll promote your bloody book, but just get me down!'

He was smiling so I thought he was still joking.

'Look, I'm serious. I'm even going to turn off this camera so you know I'm serious.'

He then leant over and switched off the video. He wasn't joking! Poor Charles! I opened the air vent for him and started to head back to the airport as Charles was busy leaning over into the back of the cockpit checking something on the video.

'Oh no, I don't believe it!' he exclaimed. 'The video wasn't working, we got none of that on film!'

He had a look of utter disbelief on his face.

'I don't care, I'm not going back up to do that again. No way! I don't care what Taylor says, I am not going up again.'

When we landed and taxied back to the flying school, Charles explained to Stephen what had happened.

'Oh well, if it hasn't come out, you'll just have to go up and do it again,' Stephen said casually.

Much to Charles' relief, however, the video had worked. It had captured some wonderful shots of Charles as I was performing the manoeuvres. His face was distorted in a look of sheer terror. Fortunately though, his screams of profanity were inaudible or we really would have had to do it all over again!

We finished up for the day and Charles said it was the

worst experience of his life. He was always one for exaggeration!

The next part of the shoot was a re-creation of the actual accident. Stephen had hired a stunt team but I said I would be able to do some of the cycling scenes myself.

I turned up at Terrey Hills early one morning at the place the crew had arranged to meet—down a quiet street that had the feel of being out in the country.

I was introduced to the stunt team. Debbie, the woman who was to play me, was a tall, leggy blonde who looked nothing like me!

I was required to dress in my cycling gear and pedal my bike around a corner and up a hill, while Grant, the team leader, drove a utility up behind me until he was very close, then he would breakaway to one side. Piece of cake, I thought.

I got on my bike and started to pedal, then I heard a loud screeching as Grant started to come up behind me. I was petrified, sure he was going to hit me. All I could do was keep riding and hope he knew what he was doing.

I winced and half closed my eyes. It was a terrifying experience.

He assured me he was an expert driver and I could have complete faith in him; however, I still shuddered every time I heard him start up after me.

When it was time to do the re-creation, Debbie had to sit on the front of the car bonnet holding the bike. At a given word, she had to throw herself and the bike off the car and make a spectacular roll in the scrub. After no less than a dozen attempts, I was sure she was going to be bruised black and blue by the time we had finished.

I was astounded when Debbie told me of the many different jobs she had done in the past. She had been a female commando in the military special services where she performed all sorts of exploits, including jumping out of planes with rifles and infiltrating military bases. She was also an expert horsewoman, and had spent many years in the police force. I had to laugh when she told me of the occasion when she was working undercover in Kings Cross, trying to bring off a drug bust. She was sitting in a cafe with another policeman, both in plain clothes trying to mingle, when a young person walked in and said, 'Excuse me, officer, have you got the time?'

It took an entire day to film the accident and by the end of it we were all exhausted. However, my bike was the real victim. We had been using the actual bike that I had had my accident on, which I had had repaired. Now it had really been through the mill; it had been tossed so many times it was a complete write-off!

The last part of the filming was to be at my house, interviewing myself and my parents. The interview with Mum and Dad went very well, but Mum found it difficult to relive some of the events of the accident and was quite emotional. That was understandable, I thought. I had relived so much of it while writing my book, and I too had shed many tears, but it was all part of the recovery process.

I was upstairs with Charles finishing off my interview. Charles had been questioning me about various details of the accident, then he paused and asked, 'Janine, do you think you would have won a gold medal?'

I hadn't been prepared for this question.

'A gold medal? Well I have. I have my two children and my family, so I have won a gold medal.'

We all just sat there in silence, until Micky said, 'Tick, tick, tick, tick, tick.' That was the last question.

It was now a matter of waiting until the story was put to air. The piece was to be called 'Survival of the Fittest';

however, Charles said jokingly that he wanted to call it, 'The Cooma Express'!

All in all, it had been great fun. One thing I am certain of, however, I am the only person '60 Minutes' have ever done a story about who has travelled with a breast pump in their handbag!

Chapter 15

THE FIRST BOX of books arrived a few weeks before *Never Tell Me Never* was to be released into the shops. I couldn't wait to see what it looked like, and hurriedly ripped off the packing tape. I pulled out one of my books. For the first time I was holding something tangible in my hands; I could actually *see* the efforts of the past year.

It felt wonderful yet odd to be holding a book with my very own face on the cover.

'Wow!' was all I could manage to say to Tim who was standing beside me. 'Wow! I can't believe it!'

The first thing I had to do was ring Mum. She couldn't wait to see it and read it, and the fact that I had made her wait so long had been absolute agony. She was on the doorstep in a flash.

When I handed her a copy I could see tears welling up in her eyes. I had suspected she might get emotional when she saw the book, but I knew that when she opened it up and saw, 'Lovingly dedicated to Mum and Dad, for showing me that through the power of love, anything is possible', she would begin to cry in earnest. I was right.

Barely able to see through the tears, we hugged each other and she thanked me. It wasn't me who should be thanked, though—I wouldn't have made it without her and Dad.

Mum didn't stay long as she couldn't wait to start reading. I said she should ring me when she was finished to let me know if she enjoyed it. I figured it would take her at least a day, so I wouldn't hear from her until the following day at the earliest.

Some time that afternoon, Mum called and said she'd finished. I couldn't believe it, it must have only been four hours since she had been over to visit. She told me she had sat down with a cup of coffee and a box of tissues and had read the book in one sitting. She loved it. She said she couldn't put it down and in the process had gone through her entire box of tissues!

In the following days some of my friends and family came over to pick up their copies. Annabel saw one of them walk out of the door with a book under one arm and she quickly grabbed it.

'You can't take that, that's Mummy's book,' she said defiantly.

Annabel had watched me writing the book over the past year and a half and of course she believed Mummy was writing *a* book. When she saw someone walking out with Mummy's book, she believed it was the only one that existed. She was absolutely astounded when I later took her around to various shops to see Mummy's book in the window. 'There are so many books!' she would say wide-eyed.

On the night of the screening of the '60 Minutes' story some of my family and friends came around to watch it at our house, and I promised Annabel that she could stay up late to see Mummy on television.

We all watched with great excitement as my story came to air. When they showed the mock accident, Annabel was very upset. All she could see was her mummy being hit by a car and it took a lot of reassuring that it was only pretend to put her at ease.

The next day the phone began ringing early. Friends called to say they had loved the story and Stephen wanted to know whether I had liked it. I had. I thought they had done a great job.

Stephen also wanted to pass on some messages they had received when the story went to air. There were some encouraging faxes and an enquiry from a large insurance company. Apparently an employee had seen the show and suggested I speak at their conference. There was also a message from someone from a speaking agency who wanted to manage my speaking career.

This was a little bit daunting. I had no idea that there was such a thing as a speaking circuit. But much to my amazement I was to discover that people went around giving talks and got paid for it. Of course it was more than just standing up and talking—which for most people is more than enough to make their stomach churn—you had to be entertaining and have a message. You had to be totally professional. This, I realised, was my next challenge!

I followed up on the phone calls and before long I was booked to fly to Adelaide to speak at an AMP conference as well as to Brisbane to speak at a Prudential conference. All this and my book was still to be released!

Pan Macmillan New Zealand had decided to publish my book over there and had invited me to attend a women's book tour to coincide with the launch. I would be required to spend a whole week in New Zealand.

I was thrilled that *Never Tell Me Never* was going overseas; however, Charlotte was only six months old and I was still breastfeeding. The tour would be very demanding and would be made even more difficult with a baby. Talking it over with Tim, I decided I would go alone. I would just have to wean beforehand. I didn't want to disrupt Charlotte's schedule by dragging her around the countryside, putting up with car travel and aeroplane travel, dreading what would happen if she got sick. No, she would be better off with her daddy, at home in her own bed.

I jetted off to New Zealand feeling a mixture of excitement and sadness. I would be away from the girls for a whole week and I knew I would miss them terribly. I suddenly felt very alone.

At the hotel I went through the publicity plans for the tour. When I had first received the schedule, Tim had commented that it was too hectic. Because of my injuries I tend to tire very quickly and often get infections, but I had insisted that I would be fine. Each day for the next week I was required to do numerous interviews with radio stations and newspapers. I would also be giving a number of literary talks to different groups as part of the women's book festival. There were quite a few visiting authors in New Zealand for the festival, but I had a lot of trouble thinking of myself in these terms. I really didn't feel like an 'author'!

We travelled from the North Island down to the South and most of the talks were to groups that averaged around fifty people, usually women. After each talk there was a question time and I was often asked the same questions. One that was invariably raised was what had happened to the driver who hit me.

When I replied that he was charged with negligent driving and received a fine of fifty dollars, there was always a sigh of disbelief from the audience. How could that be possible?

I could see how unfair it seemed. This was a man who had an abominable driving record, and fifty dollars would hardly stop him doing it again. However, I had come to terms with it, had forgiven him for what had happened. Actually, I had contacted him while I was recuperating because I felt I needed to talk about 'our' accident. He had promised to stay in contact with me and to visit me, but I never heard from him again.

This hurt me terribly at the time, but I had eventually accepted it and forgiving him enabled me to move on and start my recovery. I didn't have any room in my life for bitterness towards him, I had better things to expend my energy on. I did hope, however, that my story showed the terrible consequences of irresponsible driving.

There were many questions about my experience of the writing and publishing process. Many of the people I was speaking to had their own stories they wanted to get published. Some had been through accidents themselves. I told them to write on, regardless of whether their story was published. The greatest outcome is to experience healing through writing. If in the end the work is published then that is a bonus.

During an interview at a local radio station, the interviewer began, 'Welcome Janine. Congratulations on your fabulous book. I really enjoyed it, and couldn't put it down. I suppose you had a ghost writer to help you?'

'Actually, no, I wrote the book entirely by myself,' I replied rather indignantly. I guess I should have taken it as a compliment but I thought it was quite an assumption. I had never attempted to write something of such magnitude and although I was proud of my work, I thought it would have been pretty obvious that I had written it myself!

A proud Grandad holds Annabel for the first time.

Tim with Annabel, aged one. Her first time on skis!

Charlotte skiing at Charlotte's Pass, aged one and a half.

Annabel, aged two, diving off the blocks at Leichhardt Pool.

Annabels's first horse-riding experience in Launceston, Tasmania.

A bedtime story.

Annabel and I on a trail ride in the Southern Highlands.

Annabel and Charlotte
feeding Roger on
Grandma's farm.

Annabel on
Grandma's farm
with her 'dinosaur
bones'.

Charlotte aged
one and a half
cuddling the doll
Grandma made
for her.

Annabel aged
five with her
favourite rabbit.

Charlotte coming to
wave me goodbye
before a sea plane
takeoff.

Palm Beach, 1996.
Clocking up hours
for my sea plane
endorsement.

Annabel at age three, already computer literate.

Charlotte holding one of our silky chickens.

Tim and I with the girls.

Shaking out the cobwebs flying with Noel
in the Sydney Aerobatic School Pitts-Special.

Photography this section: Tony Peters – Technics Photography

In between all of the publicity and speaking engagements, I managed to squeeze in an unscheduled stop in Wellington...to visit my beloved plane, MUM! I had taken the name and address of the new owners with me just in case we were passing.

It was wonderful to see her again, if a little sad that she was no longer with me in Australia, but this was her home. Her new owners, Wendy and Brian, offered to let me take her up for a few circuits, but we were out of time. I guess I'll have to return to New Zealand some time to take up their offer!

With the week finally coming to an end, I realised that I had hardly had a chance to miss Tim and the girls. I was just so busy I didn't have a spare minute. Actually, I was beginning to enjoy the break from thinking about everyone else, and being able to indulge in myself for one, something that mothers aren't usually able to do.

The day before I was to leave I was to do an interview at a local radio station in a small town called Hamilton. I was to be interviewed by a man named Brian Portland at two o'clock. Jill, my publicist, and I turned up right on time and fortunately found a parking spot close to the front entrance as it was raining heavily.

Inside Jill informed the front desk who we were, then we sat down and waited. At ten past two, Brian still hadn't arrived and Jill was becoming rather agitated. I wasn't the least bit flustered—I was worn out and glad of the opportunity to sit down and do nothing for a few minutes. Besides, I somehow felt that everything would work out, and he would be soon arriving.

At twenty past two, Jill scribbled a brusque note for Brian and left it at the desk, leaving no-one in doubt that she was annoyed.

It was still raining heavily as we started out the door and

I noticed a man hurrying up the path towards us. He was in a wheelchair. I watched in absolute amazement as he raised his body out of the chair, manoeuvred the chair up the gutter, then plonked himself back into the chair. It was made all the more impressive by the fact that this man didn't have any legs!

I opened the doors for him to pass. His shirt was soaking as it had taken him some time to get himself inside and out of the rain. He smiled at me and I smiled back and said hello.

As we were getting into the car I turned to Jill and at exactly the same time we both said, 'Wouldn't it be funny if that was Brian Portland?'

Just at that moment I turned and saw the man in the wheelchair coming out through the doors. He had something in his mouth and was waving frantically at us.

'Janine,' he said, taking what was obviously Jill's note out of his mouth, 'I'm Brian Portland. I'm sorry, I didn't get the message that our interview was now. I haven't even received your book yet. Please, I really want to interview you.'

I wasn't surprised—we were meant to meet. I told him I would love to talk to him, but it was me who should be doing the interview. We arranged to return in an hour's time, after my next appointment.

After Brian had interviewed me for his show, he told me his story. He was now in his forties and had lost his legs in a train-shunting accident when he was twenty-one. He had been working on the railway and had dropped under one of the carriages to get something when the carriage ran over his legs.

In great detail he told me about his experience in hospital. It was a matter of life and death and there was no choice but to remove both his legs. They were amputated from just below the hip joint before he knew what had happened.

He had denied the ordeal for most of his life, he said, and hadn't grieved over his loss. This was made easier by the many drugs he was taking, but in actual fact he was denying his true feelings. He had never come to terms with his new self. It wasn't until he had a nervous breakdown and was hospitalised that he realised what his life had become.

Now he was drug free and was getting on with his life. He had discarded the prostheses he had been fitted with years ago because he found that they only hindered him and he could actually get around quicker without any legs. I watched in amazement as he demonstrated how he got upstairs by swinging his body between his arms. He was incredibly quick.

He had found a renewed satisfaction with life and now spent much of his time talking to others about his experience. He told me that if someone offered him his two legs back again, he would say no. He was a better person without them.

We exchanged addresses and promised to keep in touch. He said that he would love to learn how to fly and I promised that if he ever came to Sydney I would take him up to do some aerobatics. I said that everyone had better watch out—with the two of us in the air, it might be a bit of a worry!

As I sat in the aircraft and contemplated my time in New Zealand, I knew the highlight had been meeting Brian. I had two legs that didn't work properly, but I still had two legs, and they were doing the best job they could. Brian really was a special man with a great attitude and he inspired me more than words can say.

No sooner was I home then I was off again on the publicity trail for the Australian tour. I had already completed a number of interviews for newspapers and magazines which were to coincide with the book's release. Each time a journalist came over to the house to interview me, they had requested photos be taken of me with the girls. At first Annabel thought this was great fun, but after many photo shoots she became bored and the photographer would have his work cut out for him trying to get a photo of all of us together. It wasn't the easiest thing to sit and smile hour after hour, and I was starting to get a permanently fixed smile on my face.

I had interviews with various radio stations in the city and in between I was required to sit at home and take calls from stations all around the country. They were scheduled back to back so that I was taking a call every half hour; in fact, at one point I was taking a call every fifteen minutes. I was accustomed to hard training but this was something altogether different!

If I thought I had relived my story in the writing process, then I relived it a thousand times over in the interview process. Talking about myself all day started to get very tedious and I only hoped it didn't sound that way on the other end.

The first speaking engagement was a literary luncheon at Bowral. Mum and Dad hadn't heard me give a talk before so they decided to incorporate a weekend away with my luncheon. Tim's mother was also coming as she lived in the area, and she had invited a large group of her friends.

So not only did I have to get up in front of over a hundred people, I also had to perform in front of my relatives and their friends. I was more nervous than I would have been had I been speaking to a thousand strangers!

Despite my fears, the day went without any hitches. Of

course, Mum sat throughout the speech with tears running down her face. I could only imagine what was going through her mind. How unlikely it would have seemed a few years ago. I wasn't meant to be alive; my being here was a miracle. All that pain and hurt, all those years of agony and heartache when they wondered if I would ever be truly happy again, how it had turned around.

Early the next morning I left for the airport. I was off to Perth for a dinner and more radio and press interviews. I bade another sad farewell to my little girls; two days seemed like an eternity and I missed them so terribly when I was away.

After my talk I sat and signed books, surprised—as I would be many times—by how many people had stories of their own to tell. As I slowly worked my way through the queue I noticed a young man in a wheelchair. What immediately struck me was his smile, which seemed to light up his face.

'Hi, I'm Symon,' he said as he approached the table and handed me a book to sign. He said we had a lot in common and began to tell me what had happened to him. Symon was a PE teacher and a keen sportsman. He was riding to school one day on his pushbike when he approached a left turn. Just as he was about to make the turn a car came out of nowhere and ran right into the back of him.

Just an instant is all it takes to change a life forever.

The unusual thing about Symon was that he didn't fracture his back in the accident and was considered very lucky to escape spinal injury. However, when he was in hospital he had a haemorrhage in his spinal cord which caused permanent injury. He was paralysed from the waist down.

There was still a long line of people behind Symon, but I really wanted to hear more. We exchanged addresses and I promised to contact him when I returned home. Some time later Symon came to Sydney and called in to see me.

He told me he had been offered a position at his old school teaching another subject, but as much as he appreciated this, he had declined. He felt he needed to test himself in another way. I understood exactly what he was talking about. It was the same with flying—I had to do something completely different from what I had been doing before my accident.

It was still only a matter of months since his accident and I admired his courage when he told me that he had applied for a job as an air traffic controller. It is so easy to curl up and do nothing after going through such a traumatic experience and it takes a lot of strength to go out and attempt something unfamiliar. It is stepping right out of one's comfort zone. I knew Symon was dealing with many other issues as well—spinal injury affects every facet of one's life—and I understood what a big step this was. Not only that, I also knew how competitive it was to become an air traffic controller and that he was putting himself through a very rigorous procedure.

Symon made it through the preliminary interviews and then came up against one of those people who believes it is best to crush the very spirit of someone rather than give them hope for something they believe is impossible. This man told Symon that it would be impractical for him to continue with the process as he would be unable to make it to the top of the control tower in his wheelchair. Apparently, although there was a lift, it didn't go as far as the top floor and Symon would have to get up some stairs which, according to this man would be too difficult.

Symon didn't let this deter him, although I'm sure it must have put a large dent in his self-confidence. Instead he rang a doctor in Canberra to see if he saw any reason why Symon wouldn't fit the requirements. The doctor said he believed the wheelchair to be irrelevant and that there was no reason for this to stop Symon performing the job.

Some time later I received a phone call from Symon to say that he had reached the final stage of interviews. Only a very small number of people made it this far. He now had to face a selection panel. I knew this would be tough. It would be similar to the panel I faced when I applied for the air force reserves. I sat in a room facing eight officers who fired questions at me continually and I was meant to answer with complete confidence. I was lucky, I passed.

Symon didn't make it through the final interview. At first I was disappointed for him but then I realised that what he had attempted was far more important than just getting a job. He had put himself on the line; he had taken a chance even when he had been told he wouldn't be able to do the job. I knew he didn't miss out because of his wheelchair, but because there was something else out there waiting for him. He had given it a go and that was the most important factor.

Symon is back teaching now and loving every minute of it.

Brisbane was the next port of call, then to the Gold Coast and a literary luncheon for Life Education, and, of course, more interviews.

Most of the guests at the lunch were women and were there to have a good time. That made the job of standing up and talking to a few hundred people much easier. The biggest difficulty I had was trying to find a message to leave them with as I had so many. I only had forty minutes to talk and that wasn't a great deal of time.

I talked about many things—my life as an athlete, the accident, my flying, the challenge of writing my first book, my children—and finished by reading a poem I had been carrying around with me for some time. One of my favourites, it is called 'If I Had My Life to Live Over Again' and was written by an eighty-five-year-old in Louisville, Kentucky.

If I had to live my life over, I'd dare to make more mistakes next time.

I'd relax. I'd limber up. I would be sillier than I have this time.

I would take fewer things seriously.

I would take more chances. I would take more trips.

I would climb more mountains and swim more rivers.

I would eat more ice cream and less beans.

I would perhaps have more actual troubles, but I'd have fewer imaginary ones.

You see, I am one of those people who live sensibly and sanely, hour after hour, day after day. Oh, I've had my moments, and if I had it to do over again, I'd have more of them. In fact, I'd try to have nothing else.

Just moments, one after another, instead of living so many years ahead of each day.

I've been one of those persons who never goes anywhere without a thermometer, a hot-water bottle, a raincoat and a parachute. If I had my life to live over, I would start barefoot earlier in the spring and I would stay that way later in the fall. I would go to more dances. I would ride more merry-go-rounds.

I would pick more daisies.

Chapter 16

By Christmas the book had sold out and it was impossible to get a copy anywhere. The success of *Never Tell Me Never* opened many doors in terms of speaking engagements. I was quickly signed up with several agencies and the bookings started to come in thick and fast.

My first few engagements were with large insurance companies; in fact, I had a lot of enquiries from the insurance sector, which I thought was quite ironic. Most of the conferences were interstate, but I was extremely fortunate to have great support from my family who would come and babysit for me when I was away.

Early on I was booked to speak at an IBM conference in Cairns. The theme was 'A Step Ahead'. According to the notes I was sent, the first step was the start of the journey, which they likened to the first tentative steps of a baby. I certainly related to this—I had to learn to walk all over again as an adult. The second step was the step ahead, where confidence, experience and knowledge are developed. The final step was the step beyond, where rich rewards are there for the taking, with the opportunity to breakaway from the crowd and achieve something hitherto considered impossible.

I had quite a few meetings to work and rework my speech and finally came up with something that was suitable. The *60 Minutes* story was to be edited so that I would have visuals running behind me on a large screen while I was talking. Most of my meetings were with Peter, who worked freelance for AM Motivation, the company putting the event together. Peter did many other things too and I had to laugh when he told me he was Alfred the Hot Water Bottle in 'Johnson and Friends', which Annabel just loved. I got quite a kick out of telling her that whilst she had been at pre-school, Alfred had been to our house!

Finally, everything was organised and I was on board a jet on my way up to Cairns. I was required to be there the day before the conference for a rehearsal. It was all very professional. At the venue I was greeted by David, the boss of AM, and Peter, who introduced me to Richard Neville, another of the conference speakers. I then had to run through my speech in a deserted auditorium. Having no feedback made it difficult, but I struggled through nevertheless.

Bright and early the next morning, I was dressed and ready to go. Richard and I waited out in the venue dressing room, discussing how nervous we both were. At least I would be able to walk out onto the stage—Richard had to dress up like a guru and fly out through a tunnel to make a spectacular entrance. It was a very appropriate entrance for such a colourful character, I thought.

I watched Richard's speech on a monitor in the dressing room and then it was time for me to go on. I made my way through the maze of cords and ropes that hung behind the stage; it was so dark it was lucky I didn't trip over something. Finally my name was announced and I walked out onto the stage.

I was immediately hit by a spotlight, which meant I could barely make out the faces in the audience. I began my speech and was relieved to hear some laughing when I got to one of the funny parts. There really was someone out there!

I had just reached the part about the hospital when there was a commotion in the audience. I could make out that someone was moving and getting up. I was taken aback. I didn't know whether to ignore it and keep going, or to stop.

Just then a voice yelled, 'Someone call a doctor! Quick!'

I hesitated for a minute, unsure of what was happening. 'We need a doctor!'

Now I could see people down in the front rows crowding around someone. 'Is there a doctor? We have a medical emergency at the front, we need a doctor,' I said over the microphone.

All of a sudden there were people rushing everywhere. Unable to believe this had happened I stood in the middle of the stage feeling rather silly. Richard came up and rescued me while the medical staff took control of the situation.

Someone in the audience was having an epileptic fit, which I could only hope wasn't stimulated by my account of the hospital. When he was out of danger he was taken out of the room to get some fresh air. I then had to start all over again, picking up my speech halfway through. I had lost focus and knew that I would have to work hard to pull it together.

I managed it, although the speech was rushed somewhat. I knew we would be behind time and were running to a tight schedule, so I felt a little pressured. Judging by the applause from the audience, it went well, however, and I was relieved it was over and that the person was all right.

Nothing had prepared me for this! I had never heard of this happening before. Oh well, I would put it down to experience, and would be ready if it ever happened again which, odds were, I told myself, it wouldn't.

Soon, because of my speaking engagements, I was catching almost as many flights as Tim, and since he was an airline pilot that was really saying something.

Some of the jobs that came in were somewhat unusual, to say the least.

A job came in to speak to a group called the Ironmongers. I discovered that these were people involved in the hardware industry. This was to be their world conference and most of those attending would be from Europe. The range of languages spoken would be quite vast.

The conference was to be held at Darling Harbour and I was told that I would be speaking with the assistance of no fewer than six interpreters. This was going to be a first!

I was unsure of how my speech would turn out. Apparently the attendees would be sitting theatre style, wearing headsets through which the interpreters spoke. This would mean that there would be some time delay between what I said and when they heard what I was saying and I knew that I would really have to work my timing out so as not to rush. I always have a tendency to speak quickly, so this was one time when I really had to slow down.

Also, I had quite a few humorous stories to tell and I wondered whether they would work with a foreign audience as humour was so directly connected to one's culture.

I felt the funny stories in my talk were absolutely necessary. My story had the potential to be quite upsetting for many and I tried to play down the traumatic aspects of it. Besides, there were so many funny things that had happened to me along the way, I wanted to share that with my listeners, to show them how important it was for me— and anyone—to be able to laugh and maintain a sense of humour even in the face of tragic circumstances.

I arrived for the day and was ushered up to the waiting room where I discovered a group of delightful young children who were performing in between speakers. They were from a talent school and they looked like they had done this umpteen times before. They were all dressed in the national costume of every different country that was represented.

When my cue came, I made my way down to the side of the stage awaiting my introduction, which happened to be in Dutch. It was so dark I just hoped I could find my way up on the stage without landing flat on my face. On the stage I had a very bright stage light trained on me, which I really didn't like as I couldn't see very much of the audience. I preferred to keep the lights down to a minimum as I felt I was able to establish better contact with everyone.

What I hadn't anticipated was that I would get so much feedback from the translators' booths that were located at the rear of the room. As I began to talk I could hear all this muffled babble coming from the back, which was quite distracting. At first it affected my concentration, but I managed to keep on track and keep the talk going.

I was surprised and relieved that the audience actually laughed when I got to one of the first funny stories. The fact that they laughed sometime after I actually made the joke was a little disconcerting, but I got used to it. Maybe I was wrong, I thought, perhaps there were some things that were universally amusing.

The speech went down well and I was surprised when after I had finished and the group was on a break, I had many people coming up to speak to me and ask me if they could buy my book overseas. That was quite a compliment, I figured.

Not long after this conference came another with a slightly different twist.

I was booked to do a job for a group calling themselves the ACCA. I had no idea what this stood for but soon discovered it was the Australian Cemeteries and Crematoria Association. Perhaps they thought I had escaped them once but I wasn't getting away this time!

They were a most remarkable bunch of people with an extraordinary sense of humour. The gentleman who booked me said that he had to stay fit and healthy in his job because if he didn't, it was too easy to get mixed up with the stock!

When the day arrived, I was in for more surprises. As it was a conference, there was a range of goods on display. Now this wasn't your ordinary exhibition—there were coffins, grave digger uniforms, headstones; you name it, if it was to do with death it was there! While I was browsing around feeling a little uncomfortable, I happened upon a stall with lovely ornate boxes. When I asked what they were for, I was duly told they were for the deceased's ashes.

'Oh,' I said taken aback. But as I quickly went to move on they kindly gave me a few souvenirs to take home!

At lunch I learnt what it was like for these people working in an industry that most of us, I imagine, avoid. The people sitting around me on the main table told me that the moment they mentioned they were in the funeral business, any conversation stopped. Because of the nature of their work, they said, they had to maintain a sense of humour or they wouldn't be able to get through each day. I could well understand that, as I believe humour to be an essential part of life.

They were a fantastic audience. I wasn't surprised to find that they were extremely compassionate people who were moved by my story and were very supportive in their response to me. It was a delight to talk and meet with them. And I had to laugh when they presented me with a thank-you gift after my speech. A miniature headstone with my name engraved! I use it as a bookend and it sits proudly in my office.

More recently I was given the difficult task of speaking to three hundred Japanese businesswomen visiting Australia on an incentive tour.

They spoke no English, and I would be speaking through an interpreter. Even though I had done this before, I thought it would be a little more difficult this time as the Japanese have such a distinct culture, and I wondered if they would be able to relate to my story.

I agreed to do the job anyway—I would put it down to experience.

The liaison was done through the Thomas Cook organisation who would be setting up all the meetings needed beforehand. I was to learn very quickly how important meetings are to the Japanese.

Firstly, I had to send a copy of my talk to an interpreter who would translate it beforehand. Then they wanted a copy of my book so that the interpreter could read it and get a feel for the story. This took quite a number of weeks, and in the meantime I had several meetings with the organisers and the executives who also wanted to meet me beforehand. With all these meetings I became very adept at bowing!

When I arrived for the day it was frantic. People were

busying themselves and I was ushered to several different locations in succession and told that I would be collected at the appropriate time. I had asked one of my good friends, Jo, to come with me as she spoke fluent Japanese and had lived and worked in Japan for years. I thought she would be able to give me a hand with any language problems I might encounter and give me some tips on Japanese etiquette. She had taught me how to say hello and goodbye in a formal and polite manner so that I could use these greetings on stage.

After much fussing around I was introduced to the audience, in Japanese of course. I needed a little nudge to tell me to go up on stage. The feedback from the interpreters was distracting—as it always is—and they were slower than those I had encountered before. Jo had explained that it was very difficult to translate from English to Japanese and I think I was speaking quickly so that made their task even more difficult.

I launched into my first funny story but didn't get any response at all. Oh no, I thought, this was going to go down like a brick! I continued on and when I reached a serious part the audience suddenly roared with laughter. I was disconcerted until I realised that, because of the time lag, they had only just reached the funny part.

I slowed down then and began to get the feel of how fast the translators were going. Eventually they were laughing almost at the same time as I spoke and I knew I was on a roll.

At the end of the speech I received loud applause from the group. I couldn't finish, however, until I gave them my big finale.

'Domoarigato gozaimasu,' I said as I bowed to the audience.

Everyone stood up and applauded. I was greatly relieved.

They had been a terrific audience and the cultural differences hadn't mattered at all.

I was flattered when the organisers told me it was the best conference they had ever had in Australia and Jo told me she had watched the ladies as I spoke and said that they laughed and cried and were very moved by my talk. She also said it was almost unheard of for Japanese to laugh at Western humour.

Of all the speaking engagements I have had to date, there is one that is particularly close to my heart. I was invited to speak at my old university at their Annual Blues Dinner, an occasion when sporting excellence in the student body is celebrated. I had received an award myself the year before my accident. It was a tradition to have a guest speaker at each dinner. When I was awarded my Blue, Marlene Mathews, the former Commonwealth and Olympic sprinter, was the speaker. I considered it a great honour to be included with such company and gladly accepted.

I felt as though I had been through a time warp when I arrived at the university. Driving through the gates leading down to the gym brought back so many memories. So many times I had ridden my bike along the same route. I had spent so much time at the gym, teaching aerobics, playing squash and running around the cross-country tracks. Years and years of my life were tied up in this place.

As we wandered through the buildings on our way to the dining room, I couldn't help but recall certain stories for Tim to fill in some of the gaps in my life for him.

At the reception I was greeted by so many faces from the past, people I hadn't seen for years, many not since my accident. I was met by Bob Lawton as soon as I arrived. Bob had been in charge of all the sport at the university and was heavily involved in cross-country skiing. For years he had managed national teams for both the University Games and the Olympic Games. He had been the manager for the Australian Winter Olympics team in Albertville, France, the Olympics I would have competed in had it not been for the accident.

After catching up with many of the people there, Bob said there was someone special he wanted me to meet. A girl, he told me, who was a very talented swimmer. She was the daughter of one of the lecturers at the university, Guy Neumann. I knew Guy as he had been one of my French lecturers many years ago. His daughter, Nadine, was destined to represent Australia at the Olympics when her dreams were shattered after a diving accident left her with a broken neck. It seemed certain that her career was over. How could anyone ever recover from such an injury and still go to the Olympics?

Bob told me, however, that Nadine had been given my book and had been inspired to pursue her dream—she was aiming for selection in the 1996 games in Atlanta.

We were seated for the dinner and then the time came for me to speak. Bob had warned me not to take offence if there was some rowdy behaviour from the table at the back of the room. He said the rugby table always consumed too much alcohol beforehand and was invariably loud and raucous.

I stood at the lectern and began to talk. When I reached the accident I looked around at all the familiar faces and it all came back to me with a reality I had never before experienced during a speech. This was where it all began; this was my life before the accident. I looked around and everywhere I saw a face that held some significance for me, someone who had been part of my life before that fateful day. These people were in every way linked to my accident and my life.

I couldn't speak. I became overwhelmed with emotion. I had opened up so many wounds I thought had healed over.

I looked around the room; everyone was sitting silently, not daring to stir. Even the rugby table was quiet.

Wiping the tears from my eyes, I somehow managed to pull myself together just enough to get through the rest of the speech, my voice wavering the entire time.

At the end I wondered whether I had made a complete fool of myself, the applause drowned out by thoughts rushing madly through my head, but when I looked around I saw that everyone was standing and clapping.

I felt enormous relief. I had touched the very core of my emotions, tapped into a part of my past I had not before confronted. I was totally exhausted, emotionally drained. But I had moved on.

Bob later told me that they had never before had such a reception from a Blues Dinner; in fact, he had never known the rugby table to be so quiet during a talk—you could hear a pin drop.

Bob introduced me to Nadine and we had a chance to chat. I later learnt she had gained herself a berth in the Olympic team to compete in Atlanta. I was thrilled for her, and sent her a note of congratulations. She had achieved so much just to come back from her injuries, the rest was a bonus.

Nadine gave an exceptional performance at the Games. She came in sixth in the two hundred metre breaststroke in a personal best time. What more could anyone ask? She is now aiming for the Commonwealth Games in two years' time, and I have no doubt I will be cheering her on in Sydney in 2000!

Chapter 17

Now that I was on the circuit, I was meeting many other people who had been doing this for years. There was great camaraderie between the speakers and they were generous with their support and advice. As a fledgling on the circuit I needed all the advice I could get. I took every opportunity to watch as many other speakers as I could, not only to learn from their presentation skills but to be inspired by the messages they sought to convey.

So when I was booked to do a talk in Port Douglas I was excited to discover that Bryce Courtenay would be on the same program. I had heard so much about Bryce, he had a reputation of being one of the best speakers around.

I arrived in Port Douglas late and was to speak the next morning. Bright and early, before breakfast, I was down in the conference hall to look over the venue and meet the audiovisual engineers. I was standing around chatting when a small man wearing a pair of shorts, a T-shirt and some sandals approached.

I was introduced to Bryce and was struck by how casual

he was. I had somehow expected him to be flamboyant and gregarious but instead he was rather reserved. He said very few words then disappeared to get some breakfast. I went off to get dressed as it was fast approaching time for me to speak.

When I returned the venue was full; I suppose there must have been a few hundred people in the room. I was fitted with a lapel mike and then, before I knew it, I was being announced.

'Ladies and gentlemen, please welcome Janine Shepherd.'

Somehow I always felt a sense of disbelief when I heard my name announced like that. Was it really me about to walk up on stage? It felt surreal.

I began with a poem called, 'It Couldn't Be Done' by Edgar Guest, which seemed to reflect my story so well.

Somebody said that it couldn't be done, but he with a chuckle replied
  That maybe it couldn't but he'd be the one who wouldn't say so till he tried
  So he buckled right in, with a trace of a grin, on his face if he worried, he hid it
  He started to sing as he tackled the thing, that couldn't be done, and he did it.

'There have been many people who have told me over the years that there are things that I wouldn't be able to do, and fortunately for me, I didn't listen. In fact, I have never listened. You can ask my mum.'

They were laughing. Thank goodness!

I continued.

'You see, I've always been a brat, never done what I was told. Can anyone relate to that?'

I saw hands go up in the air, which was always a relief. Now I was off and running.

'I was one of those determined little kids that never gave up, never stopped trying, to the point of driving my parents mad. You see, I always believed that if you wanted something, really wanted something, and you were willing to work hard, then anything was possible.

'I was also fortunate. I had two great parents who made me believe that I could fly. They encouraged me to be the best at whatever I did, to be the best that I could be. And they helped me to believe that I could do anything.'

'Children always believe that they can fly to the moon, so why have so many of us forgotten that?'

I told my story in my own way. I never used notes, that would have taken something away from what I was trying to do. It wouldn't have been from the heart. If I forgot something, it didn't really matter because it always flowed. It was my story and I knew it intimately.

I had been speaking for over forty-five minutes; the time had flown and now it was time to wind up.

'But for every dream you have, there will always be someone who will tell you it can't be done. I know, because they told me. But I like to remember . . .

> There are thousands to tell you it cannot be done
>> There are thousands to prophesy failure.
>> There are thousands to point out to you one by one, the dangers that wait to assail you.
>> But just buckle in with a bit of a grin, just take off your coat and go to it
>> Just start to sing as you tackle the thing that cannot be done and you'll do it.

'Thank you.'

The audience stood up and started to applaud. Although I was delighted, I always felt slightly embarrassed with this part and wanted to get off as soon as possible. I gave a little bow and was relieved when I could finally walk off the stage.

I breathed a sigh of relief.

'Darling, that was just wonderful!'

I looked up and much to my surprise it was Bryce Courtenay.

He put his arms around me and gave me a hug. 'You were fabulous,' he said again.

I was stunned. I hadn't expected Bryce to make a special effort to come and hear me. That was quite a compliment. I thanked him for his kind comments and then he explained that a good friend of his had heard me speak a few weeks earlier and had told Bryce he had to hear my story.

Bryce had been trying to pick up a copy of my book for two weeks, but to no avail as it was sold out everywhere. I had brought some copies with me so, feeling very humble, I signed one and gave it to him.

By now I was on a high. I packed my bag and returned to listen to Bryce's talk. I wasn't disappointed. He was so natural, so funny; he spoke just as vividly as he wrote and he had the audience enthralled.

We were booked on the same flight home, and I was filled with a child's excitement at being able to spend the whole afternoon sitting next to him. We talked and talked. We had both been through separate ordeals, both suffered differently, and yet, from those different perspectives of parent and patient, we found we had a lot in common.

I was actually reading his book, *April Fool's Day*, at the time, which I found one of the most revealing and emotional books I had ever read. I cried my way through it and, as a parent, could imagine the heartache he had been through. It must have taken so much courage to have shared his story.

As it turned out my book was coming out in paperback

in a few months' time. I asked Bryce if he would consider writing something for the cover. He said he would be delighted and a few weeks later I received a wonderful quote from him.

'If ever there was a perfect example of the power of one, this is it!'

I was off on another speaking engagement, in Tasmania this time, when the paperback came out. Tim had managed to get a few days off work so we took the opportunity to go on holiday with the girls.

I had never been to Tasmania before but I had heard so much about its beauty, I couldn't wait to get there. Besides, we hadn't had a holiday for years and desperately needed to get away.

We flew down to Hobart where we stayed at a guesthouse for the night. The next day we drove down to Port Arthur to have a look around. It was a glorious day and we had a wonderful time wandering around the historic site. It remains so vivid in my memory, all the more so because of the terrible tragedy that was to befall this tiny town less than a year later.

We stopped off at another bed and breakfast on the way back to Launceston where I was due to talk the next day. When we arrived I was grateful to the organisers as they had booked us into a suite. With two small children it was wonderful to have so much space.

The conference line-up was impressive. The speaker to proceed me was Laurie Lawrence and following me was a young man named Nick Feteris. Laurie had a reputation of being one of the very best motivational speakers on the circuit and I couldn't wait to hear him. Nick too had a remarkable story. An avid adventurer, he bungy-jumped off the highest cliff face in the world, the Trango Tower in Pakistan. You have to be really crazy to do that. Unfortunately, I missed Nick's speech as my duties as a mother called me away.

I was enthralled to hear Laurie speak, he was just brilliant. He was so funny, the audience was in hysterics. He was also extremely inspiring as he recalled his Olympic experiences. I must admit, though, I did get a bit teary—it was a bit close to home.

It was daunting having to follow a speaker of Laurie's calibre, but I was relieved to get an equally enthusiastic reception.

We didn't have long enough in Tasmania but it had been a wonderful holiday, just what we needed. And I had managed to fulfil my publicity obligations too as I had given several interviews with radio stations whilst I was there.

In Queensland I was taken care of by the owners of the Mary Ryan bookshops, Phil and Margaret Ryan and their daughter Adrienne. They are lovely people and they made me feel like a long lost friend.

I was to do two talks for Mary Ryan, one in Toowoomba and one in Southport. In Toowoomba, Phil introduced me to everyone as they came in for the evening. There were quite a number of schoolchildren who had come along which was great. I was also pleased and very surprised to see a friend whom I hadn't seen for years.

Jack Lynch was an ex-air force pilot who had flown with my old boss Noel. When I left Bankstown he was working as a test-pilot for one of the companies at the airport. I used to hear him all the time when I was out teaching in the training area, and when he wasn't flying he was often hanging out at the aerobatic school with the rest of us.

Jack was a wonderful poet and I still had some of his poems that he had written about flying at home. I had heard that he had left and gone to Queensland, but it never occurred to me that I would find him in Toowoomba. He was also married to the most delightful girl, Mary-Lou, whom he brought along with him.

The night went smoothly and it was great to catch up with some old friends. The next didn't exactly run as smoothly!

Waiting for everyone to turn up for a talk in their Southport store, I noticed a young man arrive in a wheelchair. He was attached to a respirator and his hands were very delicately placed on a board that rested in front of him. He was good-looking and I could tell, even though he was sitting in a chair, that he was tall.

I knew other people would be thinking, What a shame. You see, I had heard it so many times myself. '*What a shame you didn't make it to the Olympics . . . What a pity you have lost so much . . . What an awful shame . . .*'

It is such a futile way of thinking. Nothing is without purpose.

I didn't pay too much attention to the young man, only to say hello. Once everyone had arrived, I began. It wasn't the sort of talk I would have given at a conference, there were only about fifty or sixty people seated inside the shop. It was very cosy.

I was in the middle of recalling details of the accident when much to my disbelief—or should I say absolute amazement—a woman seated only two feet from me dropped to the ground and vomited all over the floor.

Not again!

Acting quickly this time, I immediately got help for the woman. Poor thing had had a fainting spell and thrown up at the same time. When she recovered she was very embarrassed and apologised profusely.

I was beginning to wonder whether it was me; maybe my story was a bit too traumatic. I hoped not, because I actually left out most of the gory details.

At the end of the night, when I was signing books, the young man came over and introduced himself, in his laboured speech, as Perry Cullin. Perry was well known on the Gold Coast as a promising young footballer sure to represent his country one day. He had been involved in a scrum collapse and was now a complete quadriplegic.

I was in awe of him. He was so young yet he had a maturity beyond his years. With a smile on his face, he said he believed his accident was for a reason, that even though he was in a chair, he was going to do more good than he could ever have done playing football.

We talked about the speaking circuit and he said that he would love to tackle that one day. He had only recently had the accident but I knew that when he was ready, Perry Cullin would have a lot to offer the world.

Meeting him was definitely the high point of my book tour.

If I thought speaking to a few hundred people was a challenge, then I was about to undertake the biggest challenge of my life.

I had been asked to speak to a network marketing organisation that was having three meetings, one in Melbourne, one in Canberra and one on the Gold Coast. The meetings, or family reunions as they were called, would each have about one to two thousand people present.

Now that was what I called a large audience. But, I

figured speaking to one thousand couldn't really be that different from speaking to one hundred.

Never before having had anything to do with such a large group, I was unsure what to expect. I was pleasantly surprised. The people involved were extremely professional, and everyone was enthusiastic and positive. Another speaker whom I had recently met on the circuit, Captain Jerry Coffee from the United States, once said, 'If you ever have a problem with your self-esteem, then go and talk to an Amway group.' I was about to learn first-hand what he meant.

The reception I received at the end of each talk was unbelievable. Thousands of people standing and clapping certainly does wonders for your confidence. To feel so appreciated is quite a buzz.

I was presented with some wonderful mementos from these functions, one of which is a quote from John Homer Miller that hangs proudly on my wall. It reads, 'Your living is determined not so much by what life brings to you as by the attitude you bring to life, not so much by what happens to you as by the way your mind looks at what happens.'

Not long afterwards I was approached to speak at three more functions that made two thousand seem like an intimate gathering. They were called Free Enterprise Days or Dream-weekends and were, so I was told, going to be huge.

The first function was to be at the Melbourne Tennis Centre; the second was to be in Queensland and the third in New Zealand. Melbourne would be the biggest, I was informed. Probably around twenty thousand people.

'Twenty thousand people!' I gasped. Me, in front of twenty thousand people. That was something I couldn't get my mind around. There would have to be screens around the auditorium so people who were too far away from the stage could see me.

I felt a mixture of emotions. Apprehension, disbelief, fear

and, of course, excitement. I worked hard on my speech and I rehearsed it over and over again. I didn't want to be lost for words standing up there in front of so many people. This was most definitely not a time for stage fright.

Finally, the day arrived and I was as ready as I'd ever be.

At the venue, I could feel my adrenalin rise at the number of people milling around the building. The car park was jam-packed. It was like a rock concert.

I was escorted to a back room to wait and prepare myself. There were television screens everywhere so I could see the other presenters and I could also see part of the crowd. Now I was really starting to get nervous!

Walking down the maze of corridors, I finally reached the main auditorium. I looked around, trying to take it all in. Literally wall to wall people, it was an awesome sight.

Marcia Hines was up on the stage singing. The audience was clapping and singing along. They loved her. The place was jumping and I was being swept along with the excitement.

I was miked up. I could feel my heart pumping through my chest. I hadn't felt this way for a long time. It was like waiting on the start line for a major race. This was the Olympics of the speaking circuit; well it felt that way to me!

Time slowed down. There was a man up on the stage; I wasn't sure what he was talking about, I was so busy focusing on what I had to do.

Then I heard my name.

'Ladies and gentlemen, please give a wonderful welcome to Janine Shepherd.'

I could hardly hear myself think for the noise. I walked up on the stage and stood there. The audience didn't stop clapping; the music boomed in the background. I was overwhelmed. How on earth did I ever get here? This was like a dream.

I felt so very small. I must have been a tiny speck to the people at the back of the auditorium. I couldn't see them, only a faint shadow in the distance. I started to talk and there was silence.

As I walked slowly across the stage, I could just make out the flickering of the screen with the video backdrop. I guessed I had been talking for about fifteen minutes.

Then it happened!

I heard it, but didn't believe it at first. Surely not? The commotion was coming from in front of me, up in the first section of seats. They must be getting up to go to the bathroom. Just keep going, I told myself.

'Doctor, we need a doctor,' a voice yelled.

Unbelievably, it was another medical emergency! At least I knew exactly what to do. I called for a doctor, and stood to one side of the stage. After a few minutes the situation was under control; I quickly gathered my thoughts and continued.

I finished my speech and was overwhelmed by the response. Twenty thousand people standing and clapping is something to be seen, let alone from the perspective of being all alone on stage. It is a very humbling experience.

Once off the stage I was whisked away to sign books. It took some time trying to get to the area where the table was as I was continually stopped by people who wanted to talk to me. By the time I reached the signing table a huge queue had already formed, and I was told it was growing quickly. In fact I couldn't see the end of it as it curled around the building out of sight. I tried my best to sign as quickly as possible so people wouldn't have to stand and wait for too long, but I found that everyone had something to say that just couldn't be rushed.

The queue was never-ending. People were standing for what must have been hours. One man had read almost half of my book by the time he got to me, he had been standing in the queue so long. One lady even fainted. I didn't finish signing books until midnight and by then my hand was numb and I was completely exhausted.

If I had ever had any doubts about getting up and telling my story over and over, or sharing my most intimate thoughts, I certainly no longer did. It was incredibly satisfying to feel that in some way my accident, my story, was doing some good. This, I thought, is what it was all for. To finally be able to give something back.

The Brisbane meeting was slightly smaller than Melbourne—only fifteen thousand! I had joked that the organisers should make sure there was a doctor present. But of course it couldn't really happen again ... could it?

It did!

At around the same point, another commotion occurred and a doctor was called. Determined to find out what was causing this, I made my way to the medical room after my speech was over to find the man who had collapsed. I was relieved to find he was all right. He told me that he had never fainted in his life before; yet one minute he was listening to my story and watching it on the screen, the next he was being picked up off the floor.

Much to my relief, nobody collapsed at the New Zealand meeting—everyone laughed that it was the stronger constitution of the Kiwis!

I have no explanation for what happened other than surmising that some people must find it difficult dealing with such traumatic details, or perhaps they relate to my story on an intensely personal level because of something they have been through.

After this exciting interlude I was presented with another lovely plaque which reads: *The human mind, once stretched by a new idea, never regains its original dimension.*

My mind had certainly been stretched by an experience I will never forget.

Chapter 18

IN HINDSIGHT, I know my life before the accident was very narrow. Apart from my sport, I really didn't do anything else. I just didn't have time. I feel as though my eyes have been opened to a world full of amazing and wonderful opportunities and adventures.

Not long after my book was released I found myself in Broome on a speaking engagement. I had never been there before and was absolutely fascinated by the place. I had some free time as the connecting flights meant I was there for two full days, so I decided to take a car and drive around for a good look. I also grabbed the opportunity to go on a sunset camel ride which was fabulous, although it did leave me with a very sore back afterwards!

My sense of adventure got the better of me once again when before long I found myself on a plane to Bali to speak to another conference. I had only just returned from Hawaii where I was also speaking and couldn't believe that I was actually being paid to go to these spectacular places!

There is only so long that one can lie by the pool, so it

didn't take me long before I was in a taxi and on my way on a sightseeing adventure in Kuta where I thought I would pick up some souvenirs for the girls. I was pounced on at every moment by someone trying to sell me something. It was stifling hot and I finally managed to tag behind a group of other tourists so at least I looked like I wasn't alone.

I also managed to do some white water rafting in Bali. I went with a group of men who were from the conference group I was speaking to. We spent an hour travelling by bus to reach our destination. I hadn't been to the countryside before so I enjoyed the chance to look around.

Once off the bus, we were fitted with helmets and life jackets. I had no idea what was in store for us but was about to find out very quickly. Before we could even get into the rafts, we first had to walk down an extremely steep descent which took at least half an hour. My legs were taking quite a pounding and I was starting to dread what would be in store for us at the other end. What goes down must eventually come up!

The men I was with had no idea about my accident and the difficulty I had with my legs. As I was the closing speaker of the conference, I didn't want to spill the beans on my story, so I had avoided telling them very much about myself.

When we reached the bottom of the valley we were divided into groups. Altogether there were about fifty people, most of them French speaking. Our little group took up two rafts and each of us had our own Balinese guide.

Our rafts set off and it became a bit of a race as to who would take the lead—we were all trying our hardest to keep the raft going at optimum speed. It took the strength of one's entire body to stay balanced, especially when going over the rapids. I found it quite a challenge to just stay seated on the outer rim of the raft as my balance isn't the best, but eventually I managed to get a sort of rhythm going with my paddle and felt more secure in the raft.

Our guides could tell we didn't want to take it easy and tried to find the most difficult path through the rapids. We even managed to go through a waterfall! Further down the river we came across a group of children bathing in the river who tried their hardest to climb into our raft. They were absolutely delightful.

The finale was waiting for us just around the corner. Without warning, our guide turned our raft around so we were going backwards and couldn't really see what was approaching. Then as we drifted around the corner there was a rather ominous rapid right in front of us. We all braced and over we went. The entire raft folded in half and I don't know how on earth I managed to stay inside! Our two front crew went right over the top and into the river. Our guide had the last laugh!

At the end of our trek we were faced with the prospect of having to ascend a track equally as challenging as the descent down. I looked up at the steep path and wondered how on earth I was ever going to climb it. They had stairs cut into the ground every now and then but of course there were no railings to help me pull myself up. This, I thought, is going to be tough. It was time to put my head down and just grunt it out.

All of the guys with me took off as though it was a race to the top, and I was left floundering in their wake. They must have thought I was some sort of a wimp! It was so steep, you really had to walk on your toes, but with no calf muscles I had to use my quadriceps to get enough purchase, and it wasn't easy.

I heard someone panting behind me.

'Do you need a hand?' he said.

It was one of the last of my crew. He was struggling almost as much as me. He was a little overweight, and I could tell he was probably a smoker the way he was out of breath. He offered me an arm and not being one to look a gift horse in the mouth, I gladly accepted.

We must have looked a sight! All the way up the mountain, we were besieged by a horde of locals trying to sell us their merchandise. I was half laughing, half panting—it really was the oddest place to flog goods to the tourists!

We finally made it to the top, where the others were relaxing by the bus, wondering what on earth was keeping us. I'm sure they must have thought I was the most unfit, uncoordinated person they had ever met.

The following day when I gave my speech, I could see them all smiling, understanding now why I struggled so much the day before. And as expected, the next day I was so sore from my little adventure I could hardly move.

But I had no regrets. I'd had a fantastic time and, besides, I had made it to the top of another hill!

Chapter 19

LETTERS FROM ALL OVER the country and overseas began to pile up on my desk. I read every one of them with great interest, and took a great deal of time replying to them all. I had decided that if my readers could find the time to write, I could find the time to reply.

Most wrote to say how much they had enjoyed the book; many wrote to tell me their story, and some wrote asking advice about which direction they should take in their recovery. This became quite a responsibility for me as I had never intended to imply that the way I had done it was the only way; it was only one way, which just happened to be the right way for me. I even had one kind lady write that she had the doctor and the treatment to cure all my paralysis problems. She insisted that I make an appointment to see him and wouldn't take no for an answer.

As much as I appreciated her concern, I knew the only breakthrough that could possibly impact on my permanent injuries would come when a discovery was made into spinal nerve regeneration. I have every faith that it will happen one day, but I am not about to put every last ounce of energy into waiting for that day. I am getting on with my life and when it happens, well, that'll be great.

My friend Elizabeth was right when she wrote, referring to me, 'Think of all the love she'll reap!' I was greatly appreciative of all the letters, and the kindness I have received will never cease to amaze me. Each letter has given me a tremendous sense of purpose. I have read them to myself and shared them with my family as I have been so moved by the courage they have demonstrated.

My accident suddenly took on a whole new meaning, and I was greatly encouraged by the support I was receiving. We all need to feel that we are not alone in our suffering. I had given so much of myself in writing the book and now I was getting so much back in return.

Dear Janine

I expect you have received, and will be receiving, many letters of praise on not only your courage and determination over the last few years, but also this wonderful piece of literature that you have written ... I picked up the book when it was first released but decided not to start reading it until my break from college as I had exams to study for, and just as well.

For five days straight I was riveted. Any spare time between sleeping, going to work and life's other necessities was spent with my nose deeply buried in the pages. I must confess that I have never managed to finish reading a book in such a short period. I was just so totally focused on your story that I found myself sometimes even thinking about it when not reading ...

Yesterday morning I had the absolute pleasure of listening to you speak at the Kirribilli Ex-Services Club breakfast meeting. I am not a member of SWAP, but I read in the local paper that visitors were more than welcome. I was delighted.

I listened to your story that had so moved me when I first read about it, and once again my emotions were stirred. If anything has come out of it for me, it's the realisation of just how lucky I am. Early in 1987 I was involved in a car accident which I walked away from (so to speak) with just a broken leg. To this day I have no recollection of the impact, and therefore will never understand how I survived my little Honda Civic skidding across four lanes of traffic in peak hour, missing a traffic sign, light pole, and bus shelter before jumping the kerb.

I spent ten days in traction and one month in hospital, and I clearly recall coming home from hospital and bursting into tears because life had just continued while mine seemed to be temporarily on hold. Five months of physio enabled me to walk with a rod in my leg, and today I look at the scar as just a reminder of my second chance.

Well, I won't take any more of your time, Janine. Thank you for allowing me the opportunity to read your story, sharing such significant and important moments of your life.

You have encouraged me, inspired me and made me motivated to achieve and succeed the best way I can.

I remember that SWAP meeting well. It was one of my first ever speaking engagements. There would be at least two hundred people there, I was told, which seemed a little daunting at the time.

I was up early—inevitable when you have small children—to make sure I arrived on time.

After looking over the room and checking the mike I waited anxiously for the guests to arrive. There were other speakers around, as well as a few people who were interested in booking me, representatives from a speaking agency, and many other faces I didn't recognise. Then suddenly I was stunned to see an unexpected face.

Standing in the foyer, waiting in the queue to come in,

was my friend Elizabeth, the woman who had played such a crucial role in my rescue after the accident. What on earth was she doing here? She lived in Mudgee.

I raced over to her. To say I was surprised would have been the understatement of the year. 'Elizabeth, what are you doing here?' I gasped.

She gave me a big hug. 'I thought I would surprise you.'

'But how did you know?'

'One of my friends heard the talk advertised and I just had to come and hear you. I wouldn't miss it for the world,' she said. 'I wanted to sneak in so you wouldn't see me until after you finished. I didn't want to upset you.'

This changed everything. Elizabeth had driven all the way from Mudgee to hear me. How on earth would I ever hold myself together enough to talk? Just seeing her here brought on an overwhelming flood of emotions. Despite this, I was so happy to see her. She is my soulmate.

My stomach began to churn. I could hardly eat a thing. When it was time, I made my way clumsily up the steep set of stairs leading to the stage. I looked down and could see Elizabeth sitting just down to my right. Her familiar face was reassuring, although I knew this was going to be extremely difficult.

I managed fine until I reached the part where I was hit by the utility, the part where Elizabeth entered the scene. I could feel the emotion, the tears building, and when I looked at her I couldn't hold them in anymore.

'I'm sorry,' I said to the audience. 'I have had quite a shock this morning because the lady who literally saved my life is sitting amongst you.'

I didn't know what else to say but I felt I had to explain why I was such a blubbering mess. I pulled myself together, moving very quickly onto a less emotional part of the story.

Looking back, that talk was the most difficult and most

testing I have ever given. I felt utterly drained after I had finished, but the experience was invaluable. As difficult as it was to see Elizabeth sitting in the audience, I was so happy just to see her again.

Many of the letters I received were from parents whose children had been in accidents. I could only now, since becoming a parent myself, understand the degree of their suffering.

Dear Janine,

I imagine you have received many letters since your book was published. I hope you find time to read this and perhaps give me some direction. My daughter Bernadette (now twenty-seven) had a horse fall on her three and a half years ago, badly crushing L3 and L4. Her initial prognosis was 'never to walk again' mainly because of nerve damage. She had a good surgeon who managed to put her back together again with plates and screws and we had five months in the spinal unit in Brisbane.

Finally, with great determination and an iron will, she was discharged walking short distances with two crutches and a knee brace. From the outset she said she would not spend the rest of her life in a wheelchair. The day she was released from intensive care it took many hours of talking just to get her into the wheelchair. Her first steps were actually crawling on all fours with me holding her shirt for balance and pushing one foot forward. She gradually progressed over the next two years to walking unaided, although she looks a little awkward because she has no balance when standing still. She still has bouts of excruciating pain, particularly in one foot, and this seems to be a lot worse when she is sick from some other complaint. It is as though her resistance is lowered.

Initially they talked of removing her plates and investigating her bone fragments but as we live so far from the kind of medical help she requires it is very difficult to have a doctor who understands about spinal injury to help her. When she returns to Brisbane for her checkups they say you are doing very nicely you can go home now.

She was a brilliant horsewoman before her accident and her love of it was similar to your skiing. She is riding again but because she has very little balance and is unable to push down on the stirrups, it is only for pleasure and at this stage she will probably never ride competitively again.

Your tendon transplants interested me and in early February Bernadette is going to Sydney for a few weeks. I thought perhaps you might be able to give us some names of doctors you found helpful . . . It is not that we don't accept what's happened but pain makes life difficult for her and I believe you should never stop searching.

. . . Because of our isolation it is extremely difficult to find avenues to pursue. To give you a bit of an idea, when Bernadette had her accident it took twenty-four shifts to finally arrive at the spinal unit. She was taken by ambulance to the Julia Creek hospital, by Flying Doctor to Townsville Hospital and finally by Flying Doctor to Brisbane.

I sincerely hope you can find the time to give me a ring.

I did ring Colleen and put them in contact with Doctor Stephen. He very kindly squeezed them in for an appointment when Bernadette was in Sydney. He said at this stage it was too early to think about doing anything because she was still improving, but he agreed to review her again in the near future.

Recently Doctor Stephen told me Bernadette reminded him a lot of me. He said she was very determined and had guts.

I have been horse riding since my accident, although I was never of Bernadette's calibre. However, I do know how difficult it is to keep your feet in the stirrups when you have no control of your lower legs. It makes staying in the saddle a real challenge.

Perhaps our paths will cross one day, and if they do, I will be sure to pick up a few riding pointers from Bernadette!

I received a lot of positive feedback from young people and their parents; it was not only a surprise to have such young readers but it was also encouraging to feel that my story reached a greater audience than simply those who had been in an accident of some sort.

One of my favourites was from a nine year old girl named Erin who lived in Tamworth. She wrote to say that her school was organising an evening called the Night of Notables, a celebration of learning. For one full term, forty students would study a notable person whom they admired, then they would present their work to the guests attending the function.

Erin had read my book and decided I was to be her notable person. I was honoured of course, and more than a little humbled.

By sheer coincidence I was flying to Tamworth for a literary luncheon and invited Erin to come along so that she could conduct her interview there. She turned up with her mother and her notepad in hand. Her questions were mapped out on the pages and she very diligently wrote down my answers.

She informed me that she was required to dress as I would have dressed—probably in a tracksuit. And then she would eat my favourite meal. She was the most delightful little girl who just brimmed over with enthusiasm for what she was doing. I could see her mum was proud as punch!

I was sure that if I had a share in a flying school, I would now certainly be doing a raging business. Each time I gave a talk there were always a few people in the audience who vowed to now take the flying lesson they had always planned to do. Some had taken lessons many years ago and had stopped for some reason or another, but on hearing my stories of flying, they were now inspired to start again. Many people wrote to say that, after reading my book, they had booked in for their first flying lesson.

Some of *them* were just downright inspiring!

> Dear Janine
> I probably follow in the footsteps of hundreds of people who have written to you, but I have just finished your book and feel I must congratulate you on your courage and determination in the face of such terrible discouragement. Thank you for telling me your story.
>
> I am 61, have been flying for two and a half years and have my Private Pilot's Licence, Night Rating, and am halfway through Instruments. I am absolutely 'obsessed' with flying. I am going to the Longreach AGM of the Women's Pilots in April. I hope you'll be there so that I can meet you. Your sheer 'guts' is beyond my experience or comprehension.

Although somewhat reticent to share some of the letters, I have been so moved by many of them, so touched by their love and encouragement, I have wanted to read them aloud to people so many times. You see, it could have been anyone's book, anyone's story. It was just fortune that made it mine. Perhaps it was the right time to tell it. Perhaps it was needed.

> Dear Janine
> After reading your autobiography and hearing you speak . . . I feel encouraged to write to you.

My heart was touched when I heard you speak of the turmoil that your life has been through following your accident. As an athlete, I can appreciate some of the suffering that you experienced when faced with the prospect of no longer being able to pursue your passion for cross-country skiing. It saddened me whilst reading your book as I could feel your frustration and unhappiness at trying to contend with your difficulties. I know for myself that I cannot imagine a life without strenuous activity.

We all face challenges at various stages of our lives. I guess it was your courage and determination, evident in your struggles, that have led me to face my challenges with a renewed sense of vigour. Through sharing your experience, you have given me a new sense of courage and determination to face and overcome my challenges. Life for me has regained a new focus. The challenges are still there but they no longer fill my thoughts. I can see past them and have re-established my personal goals. I have now a new found energy and belief in myself . . .

You have given me hope for my future. Thank you for inspiring a fellow human being.

I began to receive many letters from people detailing their own achievements. Many of them would make wonderful books in their own right, and I am sure I will be reading some of them in the future.

I received a lovely letter from a young lady in New Zealand.

Dear Janine,
I have just finished reading your book and thoroughly enjoyed it. I wanted to write as . . . I found your life to be so like mine.

Ever since I was a child, I've always been fascinated by planes and have wanted to fly. I've had two attempts at flying—one was a trial lesson. I went out to the airport last November to see if I could really learn to fly. The instructor told me that there was no reason why not. I bought the Flying Training Manual *which will keep me busy. He told me that it was very expensive, but I knew that. I'm also very keen on writing, and have written a book of poems which has been quite successful. I'm really keen to write my autobiography, as well as attempt other kinds of books.*

I'm twenty-six and have had a disability called cerebral palsy since birth, but I have never let that get in the way. I'm very determined and positively stubborn in that I don't give up on anything. I have gained my full driver's licence, and have been living with a friend in my own two bedroom unit for nearly seven months now. I helped plan it, and took responsibility over supervising the building of it and seeing that everything was done the way I wanted it. I'm well known for doing everything and for giving everything a go. My friends are very supportive towards me, and don't let me stop at anything. Life would be harder without them . . .

Once again, your book is really neat, and it sounds as though you've got a really neat family. I could understand how incredible it was to have your children. To tell you the truth, your book has made me very restless. I want to get on with flying, but I'll have to save first.

I rang one of the doctors at the Civil Aviation Authority in Canberra to enquire if there was any reason Kate wouldn't be able to get her licence. He said no, if she had reasonable control of her hands, there was no reason why she couldn't. He sounded very positive. I am sure it won't be long before Kate is up in the air, and defying the medical profession once again!

I was surprised, and delighted to hear that many people who had been through traumatic accidents had caught the flying bug like me. I received a detailed letter from a young girl named Lisa. She had been involved in a riding accident when she was only fifteen years of age. She had been thrown off her horse while in a flat gallop and had come off onto a power pole. She had collapsed both lungs, shattered her elbow and fractured the left side of her skull. She was unconscious on the trip to the hospital and was declared dead on arrival. She was revived and her family had an agonising wait while doctors fought to keep her alive.

They were told she would never regain full brain capacity after the accident and that it would take two years to ascertain how much she would recover. Many years down the track, Lisa has returned to riding and has also learnt to fly. In fact, she has her commercial pilot's licence and is now striving to get her instructor's rating.

One of the survivors when Boggie's plane went down all those years ago was a young woman named Allana. Allana had just begun to learn to fly when she stepped into the search and rescue aircraft that day.

She was taken by helicopter to Prince Henry Hospital, where I had been only a few years earlier. We were in the same ward; we had the same doctors. One of them gave Allana a magazine article about me, and I heard of her some time later from mutual flying friends.

Although we were in very different accidents, many of our injuries are the same, and we have become good friends. It's a great support to talk to someone who understands and has experienced the physical problems we both face.

Allana returned to flying, despite the fact that it was very traumatic to do so. I admire her greatly for that. However, she didn't learn to fly an aircraft, she learnt to fly a helicopter. And she has just recently gained her commercial helicopter licence. She is an inspiration to many.

I still keep in contact with Maria, who was in bed next to me in hospital. She was only fifteen when she was involved in an accident that was to leave her a quadriplegic. She awoke from a coma on her sixteenth birthday.

We had a lot of fun together. We amused ourselves joking about the inadequacies of the hospital system. It wasn't important so much what we laughed about, what was important was that we laughed!

At first it was difficult understanding Maria, her vocal cords had been so damaged. The frustration at times must have been overwhelming for her. Not only was she unable to move any part of her body apart from her head, she was also unable to make herself understood.

Yet, despite her injuries, I never once heard Maria complain. She maintained a dignity that defied her young age. I will be forever grateful that I shared the bed next to her, for if I ever felt that twinge of self-pity, I had only to glance across to feel ashamed of my thoughts.

I thought of Maria recently when I met someone at a function I was attending. He told me he wanted to send me something. It was a poem, he said, that he had pinned above his desk. A reminder to him of just how fortunate his life was.

It made me think how easily we can stew on our own problems, that looking at others helps put things into perspective.

He sent me the poem.

If I can do it so can you

I've been sitting in a wheelchair for more than thirty years
And though outside I'm happy, inside I hide the tears.
When I think about the folk who gripe of things that they can't do,
It brings me to this thought . . . If I can do it so can you.

Of course, there's things I can't do, but a lot more that I can,
So I try to do these things as well as any other man.
Like a little smile, a word of cheer to help folk on their way,
You know, it doesn't cost a cent to say, 'Hey, have a nice day.'

For life is what we make it and the lucky ones, it seems,
Are those who face life as it is, though we too have our dreams.
But we don't look for sympathy, so we're ahead by miles,
Although not rich in money, we're millionaires in smiles.

The birds, the sunshine, rain and flowers, belong to everyone,
At times we take for granted the things that God has done.
So do with pride what you can do and you'll find . . . every day
No matter how hard-pressed you are, with will you'll find a way.

For regardless of what handicap you're saddled with, it's true
Just stop and realise . . . your main handicap is—YOU.
For you can smile and you can laugh, just the same as me,
Share these gifts with others and pretty soon you will agree . . .

That it's great to be the giver, so give . . . and give again,
Give your love, give your smiles, give anything you can.
For in every cloudy sky, you're sure to find that patch of blue,
And I know . . . come on, let's show it . . . If I can do it, so can you.

Colin James

There are many people I admire, and one of them is a young woman named Joanna Knott, whom I first met several years ago. Joanna is from England and had only been in Australia for a short time when she had a skiing accident.

Joanna had been skiing with her boyfriend and a group of others when she followed a track that had been incorrectly marked in its level of difficulty. It was quite a treacherous path and as she traversed across, she slipped and fell down the mountain. Unable to stop or even slow herself down, she careered into a tree which stopped her fall and ultimately shattered her life. As she lay still, she knew she had suffered a serious injury. She had broken her neck and is now a quadriplegic.

At the time of her accident, Joanna had a MBA in Business Management and was working in Marketing. Refusing to dwell on her situation, she has turned her skills to raising awareness for spinal cord injury and making a positive step towards finding a cure.

Some time after the accident, she came in contact with another amazing person named Stewart Yesner. A lawyer and a quadriplegic, Stewart was responsible for founding the International Spinal Research Trust in Britain. In 1994, now living in Australia, he had started up the Australian Spinal Research Trust. Joining forces with Stewart, Joanna was responsible for starting the trust on the east coast of Australia and now works tirelessly for the cause.

Like all spinal cord injury patients, including myself, Joanna believes wholeheartedly that one day there will be a breakthrough cure for paralysis. Just last year she was responsible for helping to organise a major scientific conference where prominent spinal experts from all over the world came to present papers on their work.

Joanna had engaged the help of Christopher Reeve who spoke on a video and gave his full support of the ASRT: 'The research being presented in Melbourne is exactly what's needed to drive us closer to a cure for spinal cord injury.'

The conference was full of hope, showing the world that a cure for spinal cord injury is not unreachable, but a realistic possibility. It is only a matter of time till that breakthrough occurs.

That, I believe, is something to hope for in the near future. With sufficient funding, and advances in medical research, Joanna and many others in wheelchairs will finally be able to get up and walk once again.

I am certain that many lives will, like mine, be challenged

and inspired by the stories I have heard since my accident. So often I have been asked, 'If you could have it all back, your body, your sport, would you give up what you have now?' Some time ago, I would have answered yes. Now I know I would never give it up. I feel privileged to have met the people I have, to have shared with so many, to have received the letters that I now cherish.

Chapter 20

I BECAME FASCINATED by many of the letters I received, drawn into the stories as if they were my own. They are personal stories, real stories, and I felt a sense of empathy with them all.

Dear Janine
I have just finished reading your book (12.30 this morning, actually) and have cried through at least half of it. Like many others, I found your story very inspirational but for different reasons, for you see, I am also a Janine who has been in a serious accident that has left me with almost the same injuries as you. So in a way you have told my story too!! Thank you!!!!

On December 1 1991, I was in a car accident in which I sustained major pelvic injuries, internal bleeding and nerve damage to my leg. I now remember so many things about that time that I have chosen to forget thanks to your book. I didn't realise how much more I needed to work through (and I thought I was fine!!!) Believe me, I have been through every one of those moments in hospital with you and I know how it feels to push yourself to the limit. I have found it hard to explain to people just why I have felt so driven during the last three years and unless they have been in that position they will never know.

I pushed myself in a wheelchair to go to University to do my teaching degree and have finished. I will be teaching next year and not a day goes by that I don't think about how hard I have worked to get there. I didn't get to fly a Hornet but I will have the lives of 28 children in my hands and that is all the flying I need!

I am still working through my compensation case and yes it does take up so much of your time. I will be glad when it is over. I feel my next hurdle will be having children. I have asked myself all the questions you have and hope I will have the same success as you. If my children are as beautiful as Annabel and Charlotte then I will be thrilled. But first, I need to find someone who loves me for who I am, not what I look like. He is out there somewhere.

I am 25 next year, and look forward to the many adventures that are ahead of me. I now feel a little more confident that it will be fine because you have been through it before me. Reading your book has been an eerie experience for me because my family also call me Nene and a passage that I believe very strongly in is the part you quoted from 'The Velveteen Rabbit' (it is pinned up on my noticeboard always)

It has been a great joy to read about someone who has the same love of life as I do and has the same drive to succeed and move on. We have both changed a great deal and will never be the same for it. I know the accident happened for a reason—mine is to teach and yours is to fly.

Well, Janine, thank you again for such a wonderful book. I felt it was my story too.

I don't often hear follow-up stories from the letters I receive, but I recently received a letter from Janine and she now has a full-time teaching job in a primary school and is engaged to be married very shortly!

I was also encouraged from the support I received from within the 'spinal' community.

Dear Janine,

Recently most of the staff at the Wheelchair Sports WA Association, and the Spinal Injuries Prevention Program and I read your book, Never Tell Me Never.

We would like to congratulate you on a wonderful story- a story of courage, determination and dignity. We all thoroughly enjoyed it, especially some of the hospital scenes that many of us could identify with so well. I found myself repeating Yes! Yes! Yes!

My name is Esme Bowen, and I am a registered Nurse and I work with the Spinal Injuries Prevention Program which in Western Australia comes under the umbrella of the Wheelchair Sports WA Association.

In 1987, whilst teaching nurses the spinal and orthopaedic course, I had a car accident and sustained a spinal injury. My knowledge and the fact that I remained conscious and I had excellent first aid and ambulance treatment, I was able to walk away from the injuries- one of the very few and LUCKY ones to do so. To be on the 'other side of the bed' was a major education for me and has taught me so much and provided opportunities I may never have had, I now have two children (four and a half and two) and appreciate so much the delightful dimension they give our lives.

I have enclosed a copy of the Western Australia's Program video produced in 1990 for you to look at if you have the time. We thank you and admire you as an ambassador for Spinal Injuries Prevention and Awareness Australia wide by telling your story to the Australian public. If it prevents just one injury from happening or makes people 'think' before they move an injured person then you have achieved something wonderful for an individual and their family.

My eyes were opened by many of the letters I received. I had never imagined that just by sharing one's personal trials, others with entirely different stories could be encouraged. Some of the letters were quite shocking, and my heart was touched in ways I could never have imagined.

Dear Janine

I read your autobiography and I just had to write and thank you for having it published. You see, I was in a sort of accident where I was very badly injured two years ago, and I have only recently begun to pull my life together. Your book made me realise that there was hope, and that I was not alone.

Three years ago I was being stalked by a man who worked where I did. He was sacked for harassing female workers, including me, and somehow he decided it was my fault, and would not leave me alone.

At that time there was no stalking law, and because he had not actually hurt me, the police were powerless to do anything. The stalking became more frequent, and he would phone me all the time or send badly cut-up dead animals. As always, the police could do nothing because there was no proof who was sending them.

I had to withdraw from University in my honours year, and I had to leave my job because of his continued harassment. And then a year after it began, he broke into my family home and killed my three cats. This time he was arrested and charged, but the bail was granted on the condition he agree to a restraining order protecting me and my mother.

Unfortunately he had followed me, and I was alone in a car park in the city at night. There was no one around to help me, and even though I tried to fight him, he raped me three times. He also stabbed me five times and knocked me unconscious. It was an experience that I will never forget. I think the worst part was knowing that he was going to do something to me, but not knowing what or when. Even now, I can still feel that incredible sense of fear.

After waking up in hospital, everyone was telling me how lucky I was to be alive. I had been found a few hours after the incident and had lost a lot of blood. The man had also been found lying with me, but he had killed himself. I was sure that I could not go on.

I guess it was the staff at the hospital, my family and my friends that made me realise later just how lucky I truly was. But at the time I was just so scared and angry.

It took me nine months to walk again, and even now I don't have full use of my left leg. My right arm is still partially paralysed, but it's improving. The pain is still there from a couple of the wounds, but I have developed ways to deal with that.

There were many times during that long recovery that I was sure I would never get better. But reading your book, and looking back at that time now, I realised that I have a second chance, and that I can use what happened to me to help others.

I have been working for the past month with a counselling agency, assisting clients with problems associated with abuse and disability. And I know that because of what happened to me, I can now understand and help people through similar experiences, just as your book helped me to come to terms with a lot of my feelings.

I just wanted to thank you and share my story with you.

Margaret

I heard from Margaret again recently. As a professional counsellor, she now works full-time with victims of crime and accident victims who have become disabled. She writes, 'The work has been very hard but also rewarding. I can finally see that what I suffered is helping me help other people.'

Margaret went back to university and finished her degree. Her courage is inspirational. 'I was able to use the study to take my mind off the unpleasant experiences I'd had in the past. When I graduated I had such a fantastic feeling of strength and accomplishment, like nothing else I'd ever experienced. I feel like I can do almost anything now after conquering that fear ... I feel that the work I am doing now is having a positive effect on people's lives and when necessary I share my experience to ease someone else's suffering. Each time I tell someone, it gets a little less difficult. It is so much easier to live with what happened knowing that it has helped others, and will continue to help them.'

Margaret's letter made me all the more aware of just how much we all need each other. Sometimes, perhaps without knowing it, we can help each other by sharing our experiences. It doesn't take much to give someone a helping hand, to lend words of encouragement to help someone though a personal struggle. The strength and inspiration I derive from people like Margaret is incalculable.

Chapter 21

JUST OVER A YEAR AGO, I received a letter from a young girl named Cailin whose parents had given her *Never Tell Me Never* to show her that she could do anything.

Ever since I was a kid, when all my friends wanted to be hairdressers, all I wanted to do was to fly a 747-400! That was until I was in my first year of high school when the doctors told me I could never be a pilot because I had juvenile chronic arthritis. I was deeply hurt and cried for days; in the meantime the doctors were giving me 100% cortisone injections twice a week in my arm and methotrexate. I began to get sicker and sicker and eventually had to be flown to Sydney where I stayed in Westmead Hospital. In my time at Sydney the doctors told me the reason I was getting sicker was because I was overdosed on all my medication and might have even died if I hadn't been taken off it.

The girl in the bed across from me also had the same as me only the methotrexate had given her Crohn's disease and she had already been in hospital for a year. That's when I started getting worried. This girl was only sixteen and had already had her lower bowel removed.

Anyway, I have returned home to my parents in Tasmania where I have seen a new doctor . . . and I have found out that I do not have arthritis, I have a plica in my knee which is a bit of soft tissue that gets caught in the kneecap when it moves. I have got orthotics in my shoes and I'm back at school permanently.

Next year I'm in year 10 and I'm going to get my pilot's licence through the local college and have already been accepted. Anyway, I thought I would write and tell you that you have truly become my inspiration and I admire you greatly.

I was touched by Cailin's letter. Not only could I relate to her fascination with flying, I could also relate to her experience with doctors. So many times I had been given the 'worst case scenario', but fortunately, I didn't listen.

I wrote back to Cailin and we became penfriends. She asked me to help her choose her subjects for her final years at school to enable her to have a better chance at getting into Qantas.

One Christmas I received a card from Cailin and a little parcel. She said she had wanted to buy something special for me. Searching the markets in Tasmania she had finally found what she was looking for. A small keyring with the words *BORN TO FLY!* engraved on it.

When Annabel first set eyes on it she asked inquisitively, ' "Born to fly" . . . what does that mean?'

'Well, it means that you can be anything that you want to be,' I replied.

I had to laugh later when she took the name tag from one of Tim's bags, put it around her wrist and declared, 'OK, I'm going to be a suitcase!'

Cailin's letters continue, and so does her dream. I have no doubt that one day I will see her up the front of a 747, perhaps even next to Tim!

One of my dreams was, and still is, to start a flying school for the disabled. Flying has given me so much, and I wanted others to experience the joy of flying. I knew what it felt like to put all my physical problems behind me and take to the skies. It is so empowering.

The big challenge was to make flying affordable. It is a very expensive activity in normal circumstances and there would be many other additional expenses, such as finding the right aeroplane and adapting its controls to suit people with a disability. I believe everyone should be able to experience aerobatics; however, in practical terms, an aircraft with wheelchair access has to be a high wing aircraft, and not the low wing type that I was used to flying.

Many people questioned the viability of a flying school for the disabled, but I was convinced there was call for one. When I was in Perth on my book tour, I was interviewed on a talkback radio show. We received many calls after that from people in wheelchairs wanting to know where they could learn to fly.

Beside, I figured that deep down *everyone* wanted to fly!

As my life has continued to become more and more hectic, other priorities have forced me to put my dream aside—for the time being anyway. However, recently I was contacted by a friend of Tim's family who was interested in a similar idea himself.

David Clegg, a retired Qantas pilot who had flown with Tim's father, was operating a flying school at Bankstown Airport. His daughter, Charlie, was a flying instructor at the school. They had come into contact with a remarkable young lady named Rebecca Sexton.

I recalled her name from a talk I had given to the Spina Bifida Association, which is a charity I am always glad to associate with as my injuries are so similar to those with spina bifida. The organiser told me about Rebecca, asking if I would mind meeting up with her at some stage.

Now David wrote to say that he had organised for Rebecca to do some flying with his school. In his typical generous manner he had actually offered to give Rebecca her flying lessons for nothing to get her up to her private pilot's licence standard.

Rebecca had enlisted David's help in trying to start up a scholarship to give disabled people the opportunity to fly.

Rebecca was a Queen's Scout and was working towards her Baden Powell Award. During her training she had learnt of a scholarship that existed in England, the International Air Tattoo Flying Scholarship for Disabled People, which was in memory of Sir Douglas Bader.

Her ambition was to set up a similar scheme in Australia. David loved the idea and had joined forces to help Rebecca out. When he met up with her she had mentioned my name, completely unaware that he knew me, and said that she would like to meet me. David arranged for me to send her an autographed book and soon afterwards I received a letter from Rebecca.

> *Dear Janine,*
>
> *I'm writing to thank you so much for the wonderfully kind, inspiring words you wrote in the book David Clegg gave me. It was just so kind of you and just the thing to give me a great big lift if I'm feeling a bit down and daunted.*
>
> *Your book was published just as I returned from the UK trip and a flying friend of my mother's sent me a copy from Sydney. The rest of my life came to a grinding halt while I read it from cover to cover and I've since loaned it to so many people who felt their lives were worthless because of a major physical disability. You're probably getting weary by now of people telling you just what a dramatic difference your story has made to their lives, but any doubts I ever had that I could not succeed with a*

*flying scholarship in Australia were rapidly dispelled when I read
your book. I nearly lost track of the book for a while as no-one
could get a copy it sold out so quickly, and it was being handed
around all over the place, so it was a great joy to get a pristine,
new, autographed copy from you and the Cleggs.*

*My big interest of course is getting disabled people of all types
flying, but particularly people with spina bifida as so many have
been dealt a pretty miserable lot in life. So with my lovely new
copy of* Never Tell Me Never, *I now plan to write to the Spina
Bifida Association in Sydney, tell them of my latest progress and
donate my original copy of your book as I know it can only mean
a new start in life for so many spina bifida people.*

*David may have told you I have had a few false starts with
my flying, but this week I went up to Bankstown and had the
hand controls fitted for their Cessna 150 and although I didn't
get airborne it was great fun taxiing all over the Bankstown
tarmac. I'll be going up early March for three days to do some
real flying.*

*As well, the previous week I went up to Moss Vale to address
the Rotary Club. I was just so nervous, but they were such a
lovely group of people, so now I've overcome my initial nerves
I'm hoping I can find other service clubs to talk to and promote
the scholarship scheme . . .*

*I don't know whether David showed you the information kit
produced by the RAF Benevolent Funds Scholarship Scheme, so
I'm sending you one so that you can see what I'm hoping to
achieve. Of course any scheme in Australia would have to be on
a much smaller scale. David also mentioned that you might be
able to give me some pointers on who to approach for publicity
and possible funding. That would be a huge help, Janine, as until
now all I seem to do is run into brick walls.*

Rebecca and I finally met up in Canberra where I was
giving a talk to the Australian Defence Force Academy. She

is the most delightful young girl, full of enthusiasm and a love of life. Not only does she snow ski and ride horses, she has recently taken up line-dancing. It is all too easy to forget she does this with the cumbersome crutches she needs just to get around.

Rebecca recently contacted me with the news that there was a remarkable lady in Victoria who had set up a scheme similar to the one she envisaged. Her name, she said, was Suzie Duncan. She was born with polio and, despite also having to walk with crutches, had recently got her flying instructor's rating.

I discovered that Suzie works part-time for a gentleman named Ian Macdonald who is himself an incomplete paraplegic and who owns a flying school. He has generously given Suzie the use of the aircraft to set up a flying school for disabled people. Despite the lack of funds, they have managed to get at least one student up and flying to the point of reaching his private pilot's licence. That is a wonderful effort.

Hopefully the program will find some substantial financial backing to keep it running, and perhaps we can all band together one day to get something happening on a national level.

Chapter 22

I HAVE BECOME accustomed to the idea that I will be in and out of hospital for the rest of my life, but I wasn't ready to go back in so soon after the last operation. However, I had no choice.

The extreme pressure placed on my feet was starting to create problems that only surgery could correct. Both my feet are entirely different, mainly due to the fact that one has had more operations than the other, and this puts unusual stresses on my feet and knees. The right foot is much worse than the left and I am forever at the podiatrist to have my feet attended to.

I roll over severely on my right leg, which creates a pressure sore on my foot. As I have no feeling in my feet, it isn't until the pressure has built up significantly that I can feel anything. By this stage it has become very painful and walking is difficult. The large toe on my right foot had become so malformed that I could no longer wear shoes. I knew it had reached the point of no return.

After another visit to Doctor Stephen and after much

discussion it was decided that he would operate again. The plan was to fuse the bone in the joint and at the same time scrape back some of the excess bone that had built up. Doctor Stephen would also remove some of the tendons and transfer them so that, hopefully, I would favour a different part of my foot and alleviate some of the existing pressure.

The problems with my knees and feet were aggravated by the fact that I had daily to negotiate the stairs in our house. My legs and knees ached constantly. Whenever Tim was home he used to push me up the stairs; he even did it when we were out, and I was used to getting very strange looks from people who wondered what on earth he was doing. Fortunately, just prior to going into hospital, Tim and I moved into a new house with *no* stairs. Not having to walk up and down stairs all day was wonderful. My legs and feet were truly grateful!

Before long I was back in hospital, going through the all too familiar pre-operative preparations. There was a mountain of paperwork, which always drives me crazy, and then I had to change into my so very attractive gown and wait for the orderly to pick me up.

As usual, Mum looked after the girls while Tim took me to the hospital. When I got married she handed over this responsibility to Tim. I passed up on the pre-op; it only makes me shake and get very cold, and I like to know what is happening. The wait seemed forever; I just wanted to get it over and done with. Finally the orderly came and I bade a sad farewell to Tim. I really hate that part.

We followed the labyrinth all the way to the operating rooms where I was greeted by Doctor Stephen. As usual he was clowning around, which never worried me—as long as he was serious when he had the knife inside me! He introduced me to the young doctor who would be assisting him, and then brought over a car magazine and began discussing different models and engines.

'Come on, let's get this thing over and done with,' I said impatiently.

'Now which leg is it again?' he asked as he picked up the wrong one.

He always feigned ignorance; if I hadn't been through this quite a few times before I might have been worried, but as it was, I wouldn't let anyone else perform the operation. I have a big soft spot for Doctor Stephen.

He gave me a wink and they wheeled me inside. I already had the drip inserted in my arm and very quickly the anaesthetic was fed through and the familiar cold, absorbing rush overtook me.

I awoke with yet another stabbing pain in my leg.

My first reaction was that Doctor Stephen had done it again. I always joked that whenever I went in for an operation I always came out with something else. I thought this was going to be a simple operation, but I was wrong. Again. I should have realised that whenever tendons are involved there is bound to be a lot of pain and trauma.

My leg was elevated and covered with plaster. I could see that it had been bleeding heavily as the blood had soaked through the plaster all the way down my foot. It was throbbing intensely. I knew there was no way I would be going home that night. Doctor Stephen wouldn't allow it and, besides, I would need plenty of painkillers to get through the night. I also felt nauseous as usual.

Tim stayed for a few hours then went home to the girls. I told him that I would be going home with him the next day, but he felt I should stay for at least a few more days.

It was hard for him to understand, but hospitals are not

my favourite places and I always want to get home as soon
as possible. Hospitals are for sick people and I wasn't sick,
I told him. My foot was just a bit sore. I can be very
stubborn when I want to be!

I spent a dreadful night stuck in a room with a lady
who did nothing but complain all night. Consequently
I got no sleep at all, which only stiffened my resolve to
get back home as soon as possible. Tim wasn't happy,
but he took me anyway, along with a whole range of
painkillers and my crutches. I decided that after this
operation I was going to have a ceremonial burning of
my crutches in the backyard.

I was glad to be home, and forever grateful that I had
no stairs to negotiate once I was there. However, this was
the beginning of my problems. It was late that night when
I had to concede that perhaps I had been too eager to get
home. My leg had begun to bleed from trying to hobble
around on my crutches and the swelling was causing my
leg to ache. I tried to rest and elevate it, but the pain became
so severe I was breaking out in a sweat and felt ill.

'I told you you should have stayed in hospital a few
days!' Tim said, justifiably cross.

'OK, but that's not going to help now. I think you'll have
to call a doctor,' I begged.

I needed something stronger for the pain, something that
I would have been able to get had I been in the hospital.
The tablets I had taken were ineffectual.

Tim carried me into bed and called a local doctor who
came around and gave me an injection of pethidine. I fell
quickly asleep as I was exhausted. When I woke hours later,
the pain was as strong as ever but I could do nothing save
take the slightly stronger tablets the doctor had left me, and
try to sleep, which was almost impossible. I looked at the
blood soaking down the plaster and hoped that I hadn't

done any damage to all of Doctor Stephen's good work.

I spent days like that lying in bed, dozing in and out of a restless sleep while my leg continued to throb. Finally, about a week after the operation, I was able to get up and hobble around the house on my own. My leg was still painful, but it was bearable as long as I had it elevated.

I had to spend six weeks in plaster and I wasn't allowed to put any weight on my leg. I know I was intolerable for the duration of this time and poor Tim really had his work cut out for him.

I had made all sorts of grand plans while I was convalescing. I wanted to start writing again, but I just felt too tired to do anything much at all. I had to cancel a speaking engagement as I wasn't able to stand; however, nearer to the time the plaster was to be removed, I had an engagement in the city which I felt I would be able to do. In truth, by this time I was fed up with being housebound and was eager to get out and go somewhere. It was funny because I was speaking to a group of insurance agents and it must have looked a sad sight to see me hobble up on stage.

The six weeks passed very slowly but finally the time came. When Doctor Stephen eventually managed to get the plaster off, after much struggling and soaking of the bandages that had stuck firmly, I was amazed at how much work he had done. My entire foot was swollen and stitches ran right up from the toe to the arch of my foot.

As I had expected, I was told not to put any weight on my leg and I resigned myself to the fact that I would have to wait a few more weeks before I could burn my crutches.

As the months passed, the operation was deemed a success—I could wear shoes again. I was still only able to wear flat shoes that came up high on the arch as anything else tended to fall off my feet or I fell off my shoes! But I wasn't complaining, it was a huge improvement.

When I finally had my foot X-rayed, I was surprised by the size of the screw that had been implanted. With that and the plate in my arm, I was certain to create havoc whenever I went through customs.

Hopefully that will be the last operation, at least for a while. However, there is the possibility of having the screw taken out at a later date as I can actually feel it protruding out of the end of my toe. Besides, Tim always says that I need a grease and oil change every now and then!

I have learnt to cope with the emotional setbacks produced by these regular operations and the knowledge that I will be on medication and subjected to tests for the rest of my life. In fact, it is because of them that I am able to cope with other, less dire, setbacks in my life.

It helps me put things in perspective. My philosophy is that everything has a lifespan and no matter what happens in life, there is always something to be thankful for, no matter how small. We need to take on the hills, and most importantly we need to learn to love them—that is what really makes the difference.

Due to my injuries my health is constantly under threat and I have to work continually to maintain a level of fitness that allows me to live the life I do.

Arthritis is a constant threat and I have been told by my doctors that the loss of sensation, in my feet and legs in particular, will cause a number of problems as I get older. The medication takes its toll on my immune system and there isn't a day that I don't collapse into bed with aching legs and feet that have taken a pounding during the day.

However I refuse to give in to the pain. There is just too much to do to sit back and let it all slide away.

I have also finally been able to install a gym in our

house—well, it's more like a room we have put equipment into! One of the most frustrating things I have had to cope with is the inability to find something that will enable me to work out aerobically. I have missed the high that comes from a really good work out.

However, I have now found the next best thing, a machine that combines a reclining bike with a pulley system that stimulates a kayak action. It is absolutely fantastic!

When Tim first installed it for me I jumped in and started to go. I couldn't believe it, I was really working up a sweat! Half an hour later Tim returned and I was still at it, by this time I was looking like I had just run a marathon! He just shook his head and laughed.

It was just like the gym at the hospital, I had no time to waste.

I have also bought a weight machine which enables me to work the muscles that normally don't get used during the day. I have set myself a program to see how much strength I can regain in my wasted muscles by isolating them.

By virtue of the way I walk, my hamstring muscles are particularly weak. When we first set the machine up I couldn't even move the weight on the leg curl. Tim had to disconnect the pulley system that controlled that exercise so that I could lift it.

Now after many work-outs I have managed to strengthen my hamstrings to the point of being able to lift the machine with two small weights attached!

The progress has been extremely slow, but it is enough to keep pushing me that bit further, to see just how much stronger I can get.

I still feel low at times, but I have developed strategies to enable me to overcome that, to bounce back quickly and to get on with my life.

I have discovered that by controlling the thoughts that

enter my head, I can control my future. My recovery has been an achievement of mind, not of body.

That has empowered me and given me a great sense of control in my life.

Chapter 23

THE PACKAGE THAT arrived this particular day was larger than the standard letters I usually received. I opened it to find a letter signed 'Darren Colston', and a cassette. I wondered what it could be. I began to read.

> Dear Janine,
> I saw you speak at a conference recently at the Melbourne Tennis Centre ...

Oh, Darren must have taped my talk to send to me. What a nice thing to do. I read on.

> ... I think I got the book the next day.
> I am a singer–songwriter and was so moved by your story, and your honesty in telling it, that I wrote a song about you. That is why I am writing. I think it turned out to be a pretty good one so I have sent you a copy as I intend to play it live if that's OK by you.
> I'd just like to say, I've read some fantastic and inspiring biographies but none as inspiring and moving as yours. I

remember with every milestone, large or small, I would have to put this book down, tears welled in my eyes, and I would feel like standing and cheering for you.

Thank you for writing it.

I was stunned.

Tim was standing behind me, watching me. I was speechless.

'What's wrong?' he asked.

'I can't believe it . . . someone has written a song about me.'

'Wow, that's great! Let's listen to it,' Tim said.

I grabbed Annabel's small cassette player, which was all we had, and put the tape inside.

I am not sure what exactly I expected to hear, but as soon as the music started I knew Darren had talent.

The words were more than touching. How could a complete stranger have got it so right? He didn't know me—he had only read the book and heard me speak—but his words captured my story perfectly.

I was overcome. The tears began streaming down my face as I wondered about the sort of person who would do something like this; I had never been so touched by another person. This was beautiful.

The song finished and I sat wiping the tears from my face.

I turned to Tim, and I could see he too was moved by what he had heard.

Annabel wasn't sure what to think; all she knew was that Mummy was a blubbering mess and she didn't know why.

'Daddy, what's wrong with Mummy?' she asked.

'Don't worry, sweetheart,' Tim said, 'she's just really happy.'

Hearing this, I had to laugh. It did sound funny. I gave

Annabel a hug and told her that someone had just done something very special for me, and sometimes that can make you cry.

I have had many offers to make a movie of my story and the option to do so is now in capable hands. It is such a lengthy process, but if we do finally manage to get the right combination of people involved, I already have a theme song in mind!

Almost a year after the package from Darren arrived, I received another, even larger, package.

I opened it and found what looked like a number of letters. The letterhead was from St Benedict's Primary School. I soon discovered that Patrick Hamilton, the year 6 teacher at St Benedict's, had read my book to his class over a term. The package contained the letters that his class had written to me.

I read them all, impressed by the amount of effort that had been put into each of them. They were all coloured in; some had intricate drawings, one had a photo attached, and one was in the shape of a fighter jet!

This man was obviously a terrific teacher.

All the letters ended with a request to please write back. I knew I couldn't do that, I had to meet the children in person. I rang Patrick and told him of my plan. I suggested I bring Annabel up with me for the day and surprise the class. He agreed, although he said he was dying to tell them.

Patrick told a white lie to the class and said there was a visitor coming who would be speaking to them about careers. They were all silently waiting in the classroom when Annabel and I walked in and he admitted he had told them a little fib.

The look on their faces was just wonderful. They were over the moon. They had read the book, written the letters and now here I was. They couldn't believe it.

As we sat around in a circle, they all questioned me about the accident, flying, writing, anything they could think of. They were all very excited as they told me of their individual dreams in life, from future Olympian to rocket scientist!

Then it was time for my big surprise. They had a song they wanted to sing for me.

To my amazement, the class had written a song for me. Patrick was also a songwriter and he had a talented group of musicians in his care. They sang their song, in beautiful harmony, while I sat silently listening, wanting to shed a tear but feeling too overwhelmed.

I then had to sign their project books and they asked Annabel to sign too. She found this a bit daunting but did a great job. On the way home she turned to me and asked, 'Mummy, why did they want us to write our names for them?'

Recently the class sent me a cassette of the recording they made of my song. It was recorded in a professional studio and the cover of the tape was designed by some of the students. The group even had a name—Ham and the Mulberries.

Chapter 24

AFTER THE SUCCESS of my Japanese speaking engagement, I began to think seriously about whether it was worth trying to publish my book in Japan. After all, I thought, the women who had attended didn't speak English, yet they had purchased many of my books despite this. Imagine if it was published in Japanese!

I talked it over with my friend Jo who had been at my talk, and she believed it was also worth a try. I had already secured world rights for my book so there was nothing stopping me from going over to Japan to see if they were interested.

I had recently become friends with a mother at Annabel's preschool who was a very talented artist. In conversation one day she had told me that she had lived in Japan for many years, working as an illustrator for a Japanese publisher. She also believed that I had nothing to lose and said she would do anything she could to help. In fact, she said, she was going to Japan on business in a few months time and if I wanted she would set up an appointment with her old boss.

I gladly accepted and quickly sent off my book and any other relevant material to her publisher. I then co-ordinated with her to buy a ticket to Japan so we would be there at the same time.

I could hardly wait. I had never been to Japan before and whether or not I was successful in securing a contract, I was looking forward to visiting a new country. Before long I was sitting on an aeroplane bound for Japan, and whatever it had in store for me. Tim was in LA at the time, so mum and dad had come to babysit. Thank goodness for parents!

Arriving in Tokyo in the early evening I had to find my way to my hotel. As soon as I walked outside to wait for my bus, I was overwhelmed by the air density. It was so thick you could have cut it with a knife. My friends had told me about the traffic and the congestion and now I knew what they were talking about.

I got on the bus and settled down for a long bus trip into the city. Along the way, I was able to catch glimpses of the office blocks that were lining the freeway. Although it would have been considered past office hours in Australia, I could see that there were still many people busy at work inside the buildings. I wondered if they ever went home!

We finally reached our destination and I checked into the hotel and into my room. I opened my curtains and surveyed the view from my room. It was wall-to-wall city. I had never before seen a city so large. Sydney was provincial compared to this.

The next day at breakfast I was surrounded by businessmen and women who were busy discussing their agendas for the day. It was very cosmopolitan. I felt out of place amongst all this high-flying big business, and wondered what on earth had possessed me to imagine I could get my book translated and published in Japan ... I felt very alone.

The fact was, we still didn't have a meeting arranged with the publisher. Kim had been unable to secure a time with him before we left, and it was likely that we might not be able to meet at all. But I had to be there to even have a chance, so here I was.

After breakfast I decided to go for a walk. I really had no idea where I was, and it was wall-to-wall high rise, so I thought I would stay relatively close to the hotel so I could get back in time before Kim arrived. It was still early yet the day was well and truly in progress. People were everywhere, in cars, on bikes, and on foot. No wonder the Japanese were leaders in business!

I returned to my room and before long Kim rang to say she was downstairs in the lobby. She made her way up to the room and I was happy to see her. A familiar face in a strange city is always welcome. She freshened up and I made her a cup of tea. She then made a few phone calls to her business clients. One of the calls was to her publisher who said he was unable to meet today. However, tomorrow for lunch would be suitable.

We had a date.

Since we had a day free, she asked if I would like to go with her to visit her friends that she would be staying with. Megan was Australian and had been living in Tokyo for many years with her Japanese partner Aije. I kindly accepted her offer and we caught a taxi over to their apartment. It was very expensive catching taxis, however with all of Kim's luggage, the train would have been too difficult.

Megan made me feel immediately at home when we arrived at her rather small apartment in one of the more trendy parts of Tokyo. Kim already had a few messages waiting for her, and after returning the calls she informed me that she needed to follow up on some of her art clients that afternoon.

Megan kindly offered to play tour guide for me, and I took up her offer without hesitation. Tokyo was a big city and I decided I would probably get lost by myself. And besides, Megan was a local, she spoke fluent Japanese, and I knew she would be able to show me some of the places I would never otherwise have visited.

Feeling quite hungry, we decided the first stop should be for lunch. I was really looking forward to eating some Japanese noodles so Megan suggested a small noodle bar not far from her house. Perfect! Kim said she would join us before making her way to her appointment.

We walked to the noodle bar, Megan took us through some lovely Japanese gardens on the way, and I couldn't help but notice a few people who seemed to be practising a type of martial art to one side of the garden. It was quite a contrast to emerge from such a tranquil, serene place and back out into the hustle and bustle of the streets just outside. I was fascinated just to walk and watch the locals. There were many school children walking around. Megan explained that some children went to school for the first half of the morning and others then went for the second shift, which wouldn't finish till later in the evening. In fact I was quite interested to learn that most Japanese children attend another 'school' after their school finishes where they are tutored for their exams. It is so competitive that they need to do this just to stay up with their classmates!

We reached the noodle bar and having no idea what anything was, I had to look at the pictures to choose my meal. We waited and then carried our bowls up an extremely narrow set of stairs to a small area where a long, thin table was located. We sat and devoured our noodles, which I found very tasty, although my efforts with chopsticks left much to be desired!

When we finished, Kim left to her appointment and

arranged to meet me at my hotel room in the morning so that we could meet her boss for lunch. Megan and I continued walking towards one of the busy streets where she said I would be able to pick up a few souvenirs for the girls. She also said it was a very trendy area and it was worth seeing as there were lots of interesting shops to see.

We found one toy shop that was like nothing I had ever seen before. It was at least seven stories high, and full of every toy you could imagine. It was so overwhelming and noisy that we decided to try for something a bit more traditional. Megan took me to another shop where I was able to pick up a few traditional costumes for the girls and other souvenirs.

Megan then took me to one of the big supermarkets to show me just how expensive it was to buy fresh produce in Japan. The prices of meat and fruit were exhorbitant— I couldn't believe it. I realised just how fortunate we were back home to be able to eat the way we did. I even saw a rockmelon selling for one hundred dollars! Apparently it was considered a luxury to be able to afford such delicacies.

We continued walking until late in the afternoon when we reached a popular bar which was frequented by many foreigners, particularly Aussies! We had arranged to meet Kim as she had arranged to meet some of her Japanese friends there. We had some tea and as it was getting late, and I was particularly tired from all the walking, I decided to call it a day and make my way back to the hotel. I had no idea where we were, so Megan put me in a taxi and I bundled myself and my parcels into the back and headed 'home'.

Arriving back at my room, I had a shower and ordered some dinner. Everything was so expensive I tried to eat as little as possible! I rang home to make sure everything was OK and Tim told me that he had thrown his back out and was in some pain. Other than that, he assured me, all was in order! After my meal, I watched a movie and got everything ready for my lunch meeting in the morning.

Kim and I caught a taxi to the hotel where we were having lunch. Her boss, Yoshi Zaki San was bringing a friend with him, a literary agent he thought might be able to help us. I was pleasantly surprised when they arrived, I was expecting a rather older and very formal Japanese gentleman but Yoshi Zaki San was quite the contrary. He was dressed in a very informal, corduroy suit and didn't seem very 'Japanese'. In fact I was all ready to bow and he just shook my hand!

We chatted informally over a cup of tea while Kim and her friend did some catching up. Kai San, Yoshi Zaki San's friend arrived and we moved to another part of the hotel for lunch. I wasn't exactly sure what to expect and wondered whether they would be at all interested in my story. We talked about all sorts of things until we finally got to the subject of my book.

I gave Kai San a copy of my book and some publicity material that I had put together for them. She seemed very interested and questioned me on the success of the book in Australia and then talked about the possibility of me coming back to Japan at a later date to promote the book if she was successful in securing a contract.

After lunch we all went our separate ways, Kim to another meeting and Yoshi Zaki San and Kai San back to their respective offices. Everything was left up in the air. I felt quite positive they liked the book, however I couldn't tell whether they were just being polite! Kai San said she would contact me if she had any news and it was left at that. We all said our goodbyes and I made my way back to the hotel.

Back in my room, I called Tim to see how he was coping

with his back. He was getting worse. I had planned to return to Australia the next day, but decided to see if I could catch a plane home that night as I knew Tim was in some pain. Fortunately, I was able to change my flight and quickly packed up my things so I could get out to the airport that afternoon.

I rang Megan to explain my hasty depart as we had planned to have dinner together that night. She wasted no time in coming over to the hotel to say goodbye and giving me a lovely gift. Kim also managed to reach the hotel before I left so I was able to thank them both for being such great hosts.

Then it was a long bus ride to the airport and a much longer night flight home. Although I had to go via Cairns again, I was fortunate enough to be invited by the Captain to sit up in the flight deck for the landing, which was a lot of fun. I finally returned home, exhausted from no sleep, but satisfied that the trip had been successful. I still had no idea whether I would secure a Japanese publishing contract, but at least I had given it my best shot. Now I would just have to wait and see.

Chapter 25

ONE OF MY GREAT desires was to learn to fly a seaplane one day. I have always wanted to land on the water—intentionally, that is! Now that we had moved and we were some distance from the airport, it was getting increasingly difficult to get out to the airport for a fly. Living near the water was the catalyst to finally becoming a 'floatie.'

The challenge, of course, was whether or not I would actually be able to stay dry. Although an aircraft in the air, once on the water seaplanes are technically boats. And with my balance, or lack of it, I knew that the 'sailing' part would be demanding.

A year earlier I had decided to learn how to sail so I booked myself in for some lessons. I found it quite difficult to stay balanced and the other students must of thought I was the most uncoordinated person they had ever come across. I had difficulty just walking around the boat when we were moored on the wharf! Despite this, I finished my course and can now sail quite competently. Now it was time for another challenge.

I rang a company that was running endorsements and booked in for my first lesson. They sent me the relevant course notes which I studied beforehand. Arriving at the wharf for my first lesson, in my shorts and sandshoes, I felt a little off. I never wear shorts these days because of my odd, skinny legs but John, the instructor, said we would probably be getting wet, especially when we did practised 'beaching'.

In his typical manner, Tim had said, 'Just wear shorts and go and have a good time,' which made me think I was being a bit silly.

We sat down and went through the notes and some of the finer points of the aircraft and John took me over to the aircraft to do a pre-flight inspection. I had to step onto the floats to check over the aircraft which wasn't the easiest thing to manage. Once we were inside the aircraft I felt much more comfortable.

I learnt very quickly that it is an advantage if you have some sailing knowledge before attempting a float endorsement, and I was glad I had gone out and done the sailing course. You really needed to be able to 'read' the wind and even something like docking the aircraft can take on a whole new perspective in a strong wind.

We did some simple taxiing manoeuvres and then some circuits. The challenge was to stop thinking like a land pilot, with nice neat square circuit patterns, because float pilots fly according to the wind and terrain, real seat-of-the-pants stuff. John made it look easy, but quickly explained how important it was to respect every landing. You can't afford to relax on landing and 'float' in like you can on land because it is very easy to flip the aircraft which, of course, would be fatal. The technique is to come in with power and actually 'fly' the aircraft onto the water. It was a strange sensation but not half as strange as how the aircraft handled in the air.

Turning the aircraft in the air was a tricky manoeuvre as the floats acted like a huge pendulum, swinging the aircraft out of balance. I didn't get the hang of it in the first lesson, but John assured me that everyone had trouble with this manoeuvre—it just took practice.

The moment we took off and headed over the water, I was hooked. It was the most wonderful feeling gliding off the water and flying around the coast. No hot smelly tarmac, just the glistening water below. We flew low-level up to the Central Coast where we found an ideal spot to practice some cross-wind and short-field take-offs. Again, I had trouble getting out of my old land pilot routine and just flying, but once I got the hang of it it was great fun.

We spent a few lessons doing some upper air work, stalls, turns and forced landings, polishing up on the circuits at the same time. We also did some high speed taxiing, otherwise known as displacement taxiing, which was great fun.

One of the most treacherous aspects of flying a seaplane is the Glassy Water approach, when the landing area is completely flat and it is difficult for the pilot to get any depth perception. In this case it is easy to come in with the nose too low and fly into the water.

We flew up to a coastal lake to simulate a Glassy Water approach and I saw how potentially dangerous it could be. We did a full-stop and John cut the engine and we drifted in the lake for a while. It was so peaceful, just like sailing. I couldn't believe the freedom of being able to fly into such a tranquil setting and then fly away again.

I finished the course with some docking and beaching and I am proud to say that I am now an official 'floatie'. I had a lot of fun and I even managed to get through the endorsement without once falling in!

Chapter 26

As the years have passed, and many wounds healed, I have spent a good deal of time reflecting on the events of my accident and time in hospital. Many of these memories still cause immense pain and even though I choose not to forget them entirely, I don't want to dwell on them unnecessarily.

I believe that much of my healing has come from writing about my experiences; it has helped me come to terms with the great loss that I have endured. Working with the pain and not against it has been my redemption.

Sometimes, often without warning, I am reminded of my accident in some way. It may be something simple like seeing someone jogging along the road, or hearing my friends talk about their sport, or hearing about someone else's accident or misfortune. Then all the painful memories come flooding back, and the pain I feel is, at times, almost physical.

I still cry.

Yet I know this isn't because I haven't come to terms

with my accident; on the contrary, it is because I have. Facing my pain and disappointment has given me the opportunity to heal, and it is a constant reminder to me that I have fought and I have won. I never want to forget that. I have learnt to embrace it.

And there are also times when I feel so incredibly grateful for my second chance at life that I cry tears of happiness. Knowing that I have been so close to death makes me look at life with a different heart.

I once heard someone say, 'Life is God's gift to you, and the way you live it is your gift to God.' I will never stop feeling that I have been given the greatest gift of all.

I often laugh at the things that happened along the way, particularly in hospital. I laugh at the sight I must have been when I first went flying in my plaster cast. How on earth did I ever get through those first lessons?

I often think of my friends from hospital. I wonder how Natalie is; I heard she has had a baby and is well. I am not sure what John is up to, or Matthew. My favourite nurse, Dave, has married Sister Sam and they have had a baby together. Dave is now working for the ambulance service and I believe Sam still works in acute.

And I often think of Uncle Darryl.

I remember the times he brought me ice to suck; when my life hung on a thread he was my lifeline. I remember the children's hospital gowns he brought in for me just so I could feel special, and I can still see him standing there, his huge frame dwarfing my bed as he held my little pink teddy over his shoulder to burp him.

'Hello, little turtle,' he said when he rang me for the last time. I wish I had known you were hurting too. Goodbye, Uncle Darryl . . . and thank you.

Adrian is now heading the doctors' television network, Good Health TV. We remain great friends and I make sure

I call him every few weeks to pester him about something. He wouldn't expect any less, I am sure! His friendship is invaluable to me.

Many of my ski friends have moved on in their careers. Most of them have given up competitive sport and just compete on a social level. I see them as often as possible and they continue to be a great source of support for me.

Time has flown. I can hardly believe that it is over three years now since I began to write my story. It is two years since the book hit the shelves. My life has changed in a way I could never have imagined.

I have recently received good news from Japan—my book has been picked up by a publisher and they are now working through the translation. I will be returning there soon to promote my book when it is released and I hope I will be able to take the girls with me.

Life is increasingly hectic, of course, but I am loving every minute of it.

Tim and I have a wonderful marriage that just keeps on getting better.

All the hard work has finally paid off for Tim, and he is now flying a 747 aircraft for Qantas. The hot dog stand has been passed on to another potential entrepreneur. I hope they get as much use out of it as we did!

My little girls are growing up right in front of my eyes. Annabel is now almost six and my little baby Charlotte will soon turn three. It has all happened so fast.

Being a parent is the most challenging job anyone can undertake. It is also the most important. I have been pushed and tested every inch of the way by two very determined little girls. I can now appreciate exactly what my own mother went through!

I can remember when Annabel was very young she often ran away from me, as most toddlers do. Of course, not being able to run and catch her, I was always yelling to someone in the distance, 'Please stop that child!' Needless to say, I got a few strange looks. I think everyone thought I was just plain lazy!

I have a wonderful quote at home which Mum cut out of a magazine and passed on to me. It reads:

> A child will make love stronger, days shorter,
>
> nights longer, pay packets emptier,
>
> homes happier, clothes shabbier,
>
> the past forgotten and the future worth living.

I am forever grateful that I have been able to spend this time with them. I love them dearly.

They grow so quickly I feel a little sadness at the thought of them no longer being little. I know every mother must feel this at times. My only hope is that I have given them enough love and guidance to take them through life's journey.

I hope they are passionate about whatever they attempt in life, that they strive to be the best that they can be.

I hope they have the strength of faith and a deep love for others.

I wish for them true, genuine friends.

I hope they are fortunate enough to experience the level of fulfilment and happiness that I have.

And above all, I hope they can make a difference in this world.

Recently Tim and I took the girls away for a weekend to the Blue Mountains.

As we drove to our accommodation, I recognised the winding streets. I had ridden this path many times before. Suddenly, there it was, the Rooster Restaurant.

'Tim, let's stop here for dinner,' I said on impulse.

As we walked inside I felt a pang of sadness. I looked around the room; I could see my friends sitting around the table, enjoying their well-deserved meal after the long cycle from the city.

I was meant to join them that day, but I didn't make it.

Annabel had left the table and made a friend. The two of them were sitting on the floor in front of the fire and Charlotte had gone to sit with them.

I couldn't help think how life had come full circle. I did make it after all; perhaps a bit late, but I still made it.

Life has changed quite a bit. I am no longer the determined young athlete with dreams of Olympic glory. I am a wife and mother. I no longer have dreams of representing my country in sport, but I believe I have achieved much more than that. And I still have enough dreams inside me to last a lifetime!

I have opened my mind up to what is possible, and I hope I have shared that with others and opened up their minds too.

I still don't have the answers but that doesn't matter anymore because I really have learnt to love the questions, and that has made the world of difference.

And with so much happening in my life right now, I still yearn for the day when I can climb back into the cockpit and feel the exhilaration of flight, to loop and spin and dance in the clouds.

For this is where it all began.

You see, once I believed that the sky was the limit... but now I know that there are no limits.

E*pilogue*

As I sit in my office, sorting through the hundreds of letters I have received, I come upon one that is a particular inspiration to me.

I arrived home late one night from a speaking engagement, feeling tired and worn out. Before crawling into bed, I went into my office to see what mail had arrived. I sorted through the pile and a small blue envelope caught my eye. I sat down, opened it, and began to read . . .

> . . . *My name is Angela Bobaks and two months ago I was involved in an accident which changed my life and me personally. I was given your book as a present from my sister and brother-in-law with the hope that your story would not only be an inspiration to me but would also help me along my road to recovery.*
>
> *To say your story inspired me is an understatement. I am seventeen years old and currently in year 12. On the 18th of July this year I was playing a competition game of hockey. I went to hockey this particular night with all the thoughts of the trial HSC*

coming up and where my life was heading in relation to career and education.

I play for NSW in hockey and the possibility of Australian representation was firmly fixed in my mind. This particular night as I was playing, a lifted ball hit me in my left temple (it was a shot at goal, so it was very hard). The impact of the ball fractured my skull. The depressed fracture was placing considerable amounts of pressure on my brain so an operation was needed quickly. Bones in my inner ear were broken, and parts of my skull came away and were cutting into my brain. There was significant bleeding in my head.

The operation was extremely successful, however distressing. To top off the head injury, I tore ligaments in my right knee and had to have another operation a week later! I had never in my life thought that a split second could change your life.

To say that I am a motivated person is an understatement.

I knew what I wanted out of life, what career, where I wanted to go to university, the marks I needed to get into my course, how I was going to get the marks, and where I wanted to go in hockey. Then the accident happened.

My life was thrown into chaos. The hospital was my home for a few weeks and my life was put on hold. Recovery was all that mattered, not the HSC or sport, just my health. I was told by specialists and everyone else that loved and cared for me to take it easy! A phrase I had never put into practice.

It is now two months after my accident and with the help of my family, friends and God, my life is starting to get back to normal. Well as normal as it can be! I am now not sitting for the HSC at the end of the year due to time lost, and I have found it very difficult to face what has happened as the life I have been living is worlds away from the Angela that existed before the accident.

I was unable to read your book when I was given it as I found it very difficult to see properly, let alone read. When I did read the book I had only been out of hospital for one week and I was determined to read. Reading what you had been through, physically and mentally, emotionally and even socially, made me realise that I wasn't the only one in the world who has felt so lost, I guess. I always knew that there are thousands of people who have experienced pain much worse than I will ever experience. Reading your story was a major turning point in my recovery and in my life. You helped me deal with all of the strange feelings and emotions that I was experiencing and I was even more determined to prove to the doctors that I could be better before they said I would be.

Even though our accidents were different (yours much worse) I feel as though your book was written for me. So many things that you write about I either felt or experienced. It may sound a bit crazy but I felt and still feel that you are one of my guardian angels. I believe that I am protected by special people that God has sent and the impact that your story has had on my life cannot even be expressed in words. I have only read your book and I feel as though I know you.

Even though I had to leave year 12 and stop playing hockey for the rest of the year, I realised that life has so much more to offer than what I was focused on. I'm not about to become a pilot though!

Thank you for having the courage to tell your story as many people (me in particular) have been able to regather their lives and strive for health and soaring heights.

You are truly an inspiration and a healer.

I reread this letter with tears running down my face. I had struggled for so long, wondering whether the ordeal of writing was worth it. Suddenly a little bit of magic arrives—perhaps from my own guardian angel—and I am reminded that my work hasn't finished.

Not a day goes by when I do not thank God for this

wonderful opportunity of giving and for all the love I reap as a result.

I have heard so many stories and met so many wonderful people since my accident; they have all affected my life, enriched it in a way that has changed it forever. They are my continual source of inspiration and my reason to push on.

Brian, Perry, Symon, Cailin, Angela, Allana, Suzie, Lisa, Nadine, Margaret, Esmé, Joanna, Maria ... the list is never-ending. My home is filled with their amazing stories. They are ordinary people doing extraordinary things. They have all defied the odds; they have stretched the limits. They have Dared to Fly!

We all need to know that no matter what happens to us in this life, we are never alone. Others have gone before us, to pave the way, to give us hope for the future.

Come to the edge, he said.
They said; *We are afraid.*
Come to the edge, he said.
They came,
he pushed them ...
and they flew.

Guillaume Apollinaire